# GHOSTHUNTING
# NEW YORK CITY

AMERICA'S

## HAUNTED ROAD TRIP

# Titles in the *America's Haunted Road Trip* Series:

## Also of interest:

# GHOSTHUNTING
# NEW YORK CITY

## L'AURA HLADIK

CLERISY PRESS

# Ghosthunting New York City

Published by Clerisy Press
Distributed by Publishers Group West
Printed in the United States of America
First edition, first printing

Library of Congress Cataloging-in-Publication Data

Hladik, L'Aura.
  Ghosthunting New York City / L'Aura Hladik.
    p. cm.
  Includes bibliographical references (p. 000).

  ISBN-13: 978-1-57860-448-7
  ISBN-10: 1-57860-448-6
  1. Haunted places—New York (State)—New York.
  2. Ghosts—New York (State)—New York.  I. Title.
  BF1472.U6H593 2010
  133.109747'1--dc22

                                        2010020570

Editor: John Kachuba
Cover design: Scott McGrew
Cover and interior photos provided by L'Aura Hladik
  unless otherwise credited.

Clerisy Press
PO Box 8874
Cincinnati, OH 45208-0874
www.clerisypress.com

# TABLE OF CONTENTS

## BARS AND RESTAURANTS  5

Bridge Café is said to be the oldest bar in continuous operation in New York City. As you're enjoying the signature pineapple martini, you might hear a picture falling off the wall or the ghost of Gallus Mag pounding across the floor upstairs.

The Brooklyn Inn is a cozy place at the corner of Hoyt and Bergen Streets, complete with a mysterious ghost lurking at the end of the bar.

A ghost named Mickey may give you a pinch or a shove as you sit at the bar of the Ear Inn.

The ghost of Elma Sands might dine with you here. If you order a bottle of wine, it may serve itself by flying off the shelf.

A traditional Irish pub with a nontraditional ghost or two, plus the famous McSorley's cat.

Mysterious fires and a glowing light in the window signify that Martha Mesereau is waiting for her husband to come home from the Civil War.

This romantic restaurant is home to the ghosts of Aaron Burr and his daughter, Theodosia.

Have a drink at the same bar as Dylan Thomas did—but don't consume as many whiskey shots as he did, or you too will end up haunting the tavern.

# CHURCHES  51

# HISTORICAL SITES  67

The Public Theater has a full cast of spectral actors and actresses, not to mention the ghost of author Washington Irving.

*Spotlight: Radio City Music Hall*    197

Famous for its Christmas show and the Rockettes, Radio City Music Hall has a ghost lurking in its art-deco halls and lobbies.

# HOTELS AND APARTMENT BUILDINGS    201

From the punk-rocking ghost of Sid Vicious at the Chelsea to the "Vicious Circle" at the Algonquin, these hotels are proof positive that some guests check in but don't check out.

This luxury apartment building on the Upper West Side is home to many of the rich and famous, both alive and dead.

Several buildings on the Rose Hill campus in the Bronx have more than just students and professors inside. Ghostly sounds and sights are part of the curriculum.

*Spotlight: Various New York City Ghosts*    219

Some ghosts have a need to possess; others just want to be heard. You may encounter both types around New York City.

# Welcome to America's Haunted Road Trip

## DO YOU BELIEVE IN GHOSTS?

If you are like 52 percent of Americans (according to a recent Harris Poll), you *do* believe that ghosts walk among us. Perhaps you have heard your name called in a dark and empty house. It could be that you have awoken to the sound of footsteps outside your bedroom door, only to find no one there. It is possible that you saw your grandmother sitting in her favorite rocker chair, the same grandmother who had passed away several years earlier. Maybe you took a photo of a crumbling, deserted farmhouse and later discovered strange mists and orbs in the photo, anomalies that were not visible to your naked eye.

If you have experienced similar paranormal events, then you know that ghosts exist. Even if you have not yet experienced these things, you are curious about the paranormal world, the spirit realm—if you weren't, you would not now be reading this Preface to the latest book in the *America's Haunted Road Trip* series from Clerisy Press.

Over the last several years, I have investigated haunted locations across the country. With each new site, I find myself becoming more fascinated with ghosts. What are they? How do they manifest themselves? Why are they here? These are just a few of the questions I have been asking. No doubt, you have been asking the same questions.

The books in the *America's Haunted Road Trip* series can help you find the answers to your questions about ghosts. We've gathered together some of America's top ghost writers (no pun intended) and researchers and asked them to write about their states' favorite haunts. Each location they write about is open to the public, so you can visit them for yourself and try out your ghosthunting skills. In addition to telling you about their often hair-raising adventures, the writers have included maps and travel directions so that you can take your own haunted road trip.

People may think that New York City is all glittering lights, tall buildings, and nasty cab drivers, but L'Aura Hladik's *Ghosthunting New York City* proves that the fascinating metropolis is also home to shadowy entities that are seen only for an instant before they disappear into the rush of humanity that is New York City. This book is a spine-tingling trip through the city's various boroughs with stops at taverns and bars, theaters and parks, churches, historic sites, and cemeteries, all of them haunted. Ride shotgun with L'Aura Hladik as she seeks out soldier ghosts at Fort Wadsworth and the spirits of poor, sick immigrants who died at Ellis Island while seeking new lives in America. Travel with her to the White Horse Tavern, where the ghost of Welsh poet Dylan Thomas may buy you a drink, or sit for a spell in the Old Bermuda Inn and watch for the ghostly Martha to greet you from the staircase. And who is the rude spirit that calls out to visitors at the Morris-Jumel House in Manhattan, warning them to leave at once? Hang on tight; *Ghosthunting New York City* is a scary ride.

But once you've finished reading this book, don't unbuckle your seatbelt. There are still forty-nine states left for your haunted road trip! See you on the road!

John Kachuba
Editor, *America's Haunted Road Trip*

# Introduction

"I want to be a part of it! New York! New York!"
—lyricist Fred Ebb in Sinatra's signature song, "New York, New York"

NEW YORK CITY! What more can I say? This is *the* international travel destination. It's immortalized in songs, movies, plays, and stand-up comedy routines. It's fascinating, captivating, and exhilarating. It's no wonder the city is haunted. What ghost wouldn't want to hang around this town? Just as iPhone ads claim, "There's an app for that," New York City can say, "There's a ghost for that." Whether you enjoy theaters, parks, comfortable bars, or fine restaurants, you're in luck in New York City if your other hobby is ghosthunting.

I should warn you that not all the destinations in this book permit full-blown paranormal investigations. So, for example, don't arrive at the New Amsterdam Theater to see *Mary Poppins* with your night-vision goggles, laptop computer, and DVR system, because most theaters do not allow recording devices of any kind. At such places, you'll have to go "old school," which in the ghosthunting field means operating covertly. Instead of taking pictures or video recordings (especially taboo while the show is in progress), keep a digital audio recorder in your breast pocket or purse, and excuse yourself to the restroom after the performance starts. Once outside the auditorium, you can take some readings with your EMF meter or attempt to record some EVPs with your digital recorder, but take care not to call attention to yourself. Also, be mindful of the staggering price audience members have paid to see the show, and do not trek back and forth repeatedly between your seat and the lobby.

Other venues such as bars and restaurants may be more receptive than theaters to paranormal investigations. However, what's permitted or not permitted is entirely at the management's discretion. Please do not show up demanding to investigate a place because you read about it in this book. Instead, fly below the radar. Have a drink at the bar, or dinner at the restaurant. Then when you take a few pictures, no one will suspect you are ghosthunting (unless they notice that you're aiming the camera at the ceiling and not at your dinner guests). Going "old school" has its advantages: Relying on your senses will make you a better observer of subtleties that an EMF detector would miss, and it will sharpen your powers of deduction as you draw conclusions from information you have gathered.

If, however, you want to decloak and conduct a paranormal investigation, ask respectfully for permission. I can't stress this enough: You aren't entitled to bulldoze your way into an investigation just because a location is mentioned in this book. Use finesse: Strike up a conversation about the ghosts with the bartender or waitress, and, if you are polite and pleasant, you might be able to work your way up to the manager and get permission for an after-hours investigation. Just be aware that at restaurants and bars, "after hours" might mean 4:00 A.M.

Some New York City locations, such as public parks and Times Square, are so noisy and crowded that it's difficult to record audio or video. Still, if you can find a spot that's sheltered from the noise of traffic and the nonstop flow of pedestrians, try to collect some EVPs. Ghosts in New York City are probably brazen enough to get close to the microphone and speak!

I enjoyed visiting and investigating the locations in this book primarily because of the people I met. There's a stereotype attached to New Yorkers that says they are detached, aloof, or unconcerned with what's going on around them. It's true that they have an edge and an attitude that is unmistakably New York, but for the most part, New Yorkers are affable people. And they're often fascinating. Barbara, a docent I met at the Morris-Jumel Mansion, knew that place inside and out. She engaged young visitors with a quiz, and she was right at home talking about the ghosts of the mansion. Kenneth Leslie, a security guard at the Public Theater, was an amazing historian—I could not believe how much information he stored in his cranium. He was intrigued by the ghosts of the theater, but *dead* set against working late at night.

I love the old mansions where you're allowed to wander at your own pace. My visit to Van Cortlandt House was a ghost-hunter's coup in that my team leader and I had the whole place to ourselves. Of course, we were there on a Wednesday, but if you can take a vacation day mid-week, it's well worth it. Plus, the Van Cortlandt house offers free admission on Wednesdays.

By the way, if you're driving in New York City, make sure you do not enter a "grid" (an intersection) unless you can get through before the light changes. Causing gridlock is a ticketable offense. Right turns on red are not allowed given the large numbers of pedestrians, and there is no speed limit given the huge amount of traffic. Cabbies know this, hence their amazing ability to go fifty feet at a speed of fifty miles an hour.

You can plan your ghosthunting trip by topic or by geographical area. For instance, you might visit SoHo and the Village one day, then spend the next day on Staten Island or in the Bronx. Or set up a paranormal pub crawl to McSorley's, the Ear Inn, and the Bridge Café. *Ghosthunting New York City* puts in your hands a wealth of historical and haunted information about key sites around this wonderful city. You're sure to discover even more.

Happy hunting!

# Bars and Restaurants

# CHAPTER 1

# The Bridge Café

THE BRIDGE CAFÉ, located at 279 Water Street just below the Brooklyn Bridge on the Manhattan side, is the oldest wooden building in New York City. In 2005, *New York* Magazine included Bridge Café in its list of "Top Five Historic Bars in New York City." The building has seen many incarnations, ranging from a grocery store to a brothel. In fact, the Census of 1860 listed the residents of this address as "six Irish prostitutes." Yet

Bridge Café has managed to sell liquor and food continuously since 1794, making it the oldest bar in continuous operation in New York City.

In the early 1800s, a six-foot-tall Irishwoman named Gallus Mag was the bouncer everyone feared at the bar then named Hole-in-the-Wall. Her specialty was to haul unruly patrons out the door by their ears—with her teeth. Sometimes she overindulged and bit the ear off; other times, she hacked it off using a carving knife. She kept these "gentle reminders" in pickle jars on the bar. This gory bit of history was depicted in the 2002 film *Gangs of New York*.

The McCormack family bought the building in 1922 and survived Prohibition by operating as a restaurant but offering "cider" and beer via the local bootlegger, Charlie Brennan. The Weprin family assumed ownership of the building in 1979. They upgraded the menu and the restaurant and renamed it the Bridge Café. When Adam Weprin's father passed away in 1996, Adam took the helm as manager.

I spoke with Joseph Kunst, Executive Chef at the Bridge Café. He's worked there for six years and has had his share of ghostly encounters. Joseph's office is on the second floor, but he prefers to do his paperwork at the bar or seated at a table by the waiters' service area. Four years ago, he had to retrieve something from his office. His daughter, who was about sixteen or seventeen at the time, was there and went with him. While Joseph was searching through items on his desk, they heard heavy footsteps on the third floor above them. Joseph told me that the third floor is not used at all, nor even accessed by anyone, because large parts of the floor are missing and the remaining parts are not safe enough to walk on. Joseph and his daughter made a hasty exit, and to this day Joseph avoids the second floor as much as possible.

Pictures at Bridge Café have been known to fly off one wall and smash against another wall. On one such occasion the framed Zagat certificate in the front window, along with the *Wine Spectator* award and other awards, levitated over the planters behind the window and landed four feet away on the floor. Joseph said he was at the bar talking with a couple of customers. They heard the crash and had to look around to figure out where the noise came from. There was no one near the front of the restaurant or the window.

Paranormal scents infuse the charming restaurant, then leave as quickly as they're detected. Lavender and other fragrances have occurred. In fact, Adam Weprin, owner and manager of the Bridge Café, said that recently he and a couple of employees were standing at the bar when what felt like a silk scarf dragged across each person's shoulders, leaving the trailing scent of lavender. "As fast as we felt it and smelled it, it was gone," Adam said. This paranormal scent most likely harkens from the brothel days of the restaurant; in the 1850s, "ladies of the evening" doused themselves in lavender since bathing was not a daily occurrence. Waitresses at Bridge Café have smelled lavender in the changing room. They, like Adam, report that the scent is there for a moment, then gone. Another smell noticed occasionally here is cigar, cigarette or pipe smoke. Smoking is illegal in bars and restaurants in New York City, but the ghosts don't seem to care.

Joseph, the executive chef, remembered another incident when he was working at table one while a couple dined at table eleven. The woman went to the restroom. Meanwhile, the man leaned over toward Joseph and struck up a conversation about the ghosts of the restaurant. Joseph entertained the man's query, telling him about the footsteps he'd heard on the third floor and about the pictures flying off the walls. When the woman returned from the restroom, the man said, "Honey, it's true.

This place does have ghosts." She looked at him and at Joseph and said, "That would explain what just happened in the ladies' room. I was combing my hair and looking in the mirror when I got the feeling someone was standing in back of me. It was so strong that I actually turned around to look." Of course, no one was there, but the experience was unnerving enough that she skipped the rest of her primping and returned to her table.

Joseph told me that, on those rare occasions when he must venture up to the second floor, he says out loud when he gets to the top of the stairs, "Let me do what I have to do. I won't bother you and you won't bother me, and everything will be fine."

Owner Adam Weprin has had two distinct experiences with the heavy footsteps. The first was when he was twenty-two years old and had been entrusted to lock up the restaurant for the night. He couldn't resist inviting a couple of friends who lived nearby to have a beer with him. Around 11:30 P.M., they were enjoying their first beer; as Adam put it, "We were by no means drunk." The restaurant was closed and the gate was locked, but the alarm was not set. When Adam and his friends heard footsteps on the third floor, they ran out of the restaurant, leaving the beers on the bar. Adam's second encounter with the footsteps was on September 13, 2001, after the collapse of the World Trade Center towers. Adam and a rescue worker went to the Bridge Café, which was closed at the time, to gather food to donate to the rescuers. Adam said he could tell the worker accompanying him was tired and depressed, so to cheer her up, he offered her a glass of wine at the bar. They both needed the break before returning with the supplies to Ground Zero. Suddenly, they heard the footsteps on the third floor. The rescue worker looked at Adam and said, "I thought we were alone." They grabbed the box of supplies and finished drinking the wine out in front of the restaurant.

I had the opportunity to speak with Adam via phone on April 16, 2010. He had just had another paranormal experience prior to my call. While in his office on the second floor, he heard a yawn coming from the changing room, which is also on the second floor. He went downstairs and asked the staff if anyone had recently been in the changing room, and Joseph confirmed that everyone had been downstairs the whole time. For Adam, this ranks high up among the many "Huh, that's weird" moments he's had at the Bridge Café. He hasn't been scared since 2001, when he last heard the footsteps. He has reached a point of acceptance regarding these events that make one stop and wonder. He's not frightened or upset by them anymore.

Adam told me about the time the Travel Channel sent a crew to the Café to film for one of their shows. The crew were there to highlight the restaurant for its menu and the age and history of the building; they knew nothing about the place being haunted, and Adam didn't bring it up. "It was a hot August day," Adam told me, "and there was no air moving at all. The producer asked if they could film on the second floor where the brothel once was, so I brought him and the cameraman up there. The upstairs was beyond hot, so we opened windows to get some air. It didn't help, so the producer and I went to the roof to get what little air we could while the cameraman continued to film on the second floor. Minutes later, the cameraman came rushing up to find us on the roof. He was visibly shaken. He asked, 'Is this place haunted?' and wanted to know how the producer had whispered in his ear and disappeared so quickly." Adam explained to me that the cameraman was six feet five inches tall, while the producer was much shorter in stature, so the only way the producer could have whispered into the cameraman's ear would have been with the aid of a stepladder. Adam confessed to the cameraman that "certain things happen here," and the cameraman told the rest of his story. While alone on the second floor, he'd heard a whisper in his ear. He looked around but didn't see anyone and dismissed it. Then he heard it again, louder. He couldn't discern what was being said, only that it was a man's voice, so he assumed it was his producer talking to him. When he looked around again and still saw no one there, he became terrified and ran to find the others on the roof. Adam said that even though he could sympathize with the cameraman's fright, it was still a bit comical given that the man could have been a linebacker for any team in the NFL.

On another occasion, Adam locked up the restaurant around 3:30 A.M. When the cook and staff arrived about four hours later to prepare for the Sunday brunch crowd, they found a mess. The container that holds the base for the Café's signature pineapple martini had been emptied all over the bar. Several liquor bottles had been broken, also, including one of Grand Marnier. The workers laughed and cleaned up the mess, thinking their boss must have had a wild party the night before. When Adam arrived later that day, his cook was still giggling. "What's so funny?" Adam asked him. The cook explained the mess the crew had found that morning, and he asked Adam if he was still hung over from his party. Adam assured him that there had been no party. The cook stopped giggling.

I have to add here that everything I've written in this chapter about my telephone conversation with Adam is from memory. When I conduct interviews by telephone, I always record them using a digital device that plugs into the phone. However, when I interviewed Adam, only my side of the conversation was recorded. During our conversation I'd had the feeling that something was wrong; in fact, I checked the recorder twice to make sure it was working. It appeared to be functioning properly; the "REC" indicator was flashing, and the clock counter that displays the recording time was advancing. There was plenty of battery power, too. But when I went to transfer the file from the device to my computer, I found that only my voice had been recorded. It seems the ghosts of the Bridge Café had something to say about my interviewing Adam; I don't know what their objection was, as they didn't leave an EVP. It's especially puzzling because I've recorded countless interviews with this device and had no other problems—except for my interview with Joseph, the executive chef. His recording had an annoying buzz in the background, but I attributed that to his cell phone.

According to the Bridge Café's Web site, the Eastern Paranormal Investigation Center (EPIC) conducted a formal investigation at the restaurant in August 2007. In a video clip from *News 4 New York*, Laura Pennace of EPIC states that she captured an EVP of a woman whispering, "I'm here." Adam told me EPIC has investigated the restaurant twice, and although they captured the EVP and some bizarre temperature readings, they concluded the place was not haunted. I think that conclusion was highly conservative, especially after what happened to my phone interview.

Chef Joseph is inclined to believe the Bridge Café is haunted, even if the activity is not a daily occurrence. "It's happened enough to where I can't ignore it, even though I don't understand it," he explained. Adam describes himself as basically "paranormally well adjusted," and most patrons are clueless unless they've read about it on the Bridge Café Web site.

It's definitely worth a trip to the Bridge Café to see if the ghost of Gallus Mag, the bouncer who kept rowdy patrons' ears, is on the rampage. Maybe you'll feel a pinch or tug on your ear. Perhaps a picture will levitate or simply fly off the wall before it smashes on the floor. Have your digital audio recorder ready to capture an EVP of the heavy footsteps, if the sound level in the bar permits. While you're waiting for that, wash down one of the Bridge Café's famous soft-shell crab sandwiches with a pineapple martini.

# CHAPTER 2

# Brooklyn Inn

THE BROOKLYN INN is a tasteful and cozy bar nestled on the corner of Hoyt and Bergen Streets in Brooklyn. The building dates back to the late nineteenth century. In 1957, its owners received a Certificate of Occupancy for a bar and restaurant on the first floor along with one apartment on each of the two upper floors. When the bar changed ownership again in May 2007, rumors spread on various blogs that the Brooklyn Inn would soon close down or, worse, become a bistro. Jason Furlani, manager of the Brooklyn Inn, set the record straight in a blog response, and thankfully this bar, a place of refuge for many loyal patrons, is still in operation. In 2008, the building was seen on the CW Network show *Gossip Girl* in an episode which appeared to mirror the events surrounding the change of ownership in 2007.

This is a bar, plain and simple. The former kitchen, as small as it was, has been removed to make space for a couple of tables and chairs for those who like to sit and enjoy their drinks when there is no room at the bar. I visited the Brooklyn Inn in 2009 and met with Kevin Bohl, one of the bartenders, whom I have known since my high school days. Kevin works at the Brooklyn Inn three nights a week.

One spring night in 2008, when Kevin had been pouring drinks at the Brooklyn Inn for three years, Kevin encountered a spirit of the paranormal kind. At first, nothing seemed out of the ordinary as Kevin worked his shift. "It was around 11 P.M. and the bar was packed," he said.

I should note that, at this time, the space just beyond the bar was still a kitchen. Kevin always kept a keen eye on that area while tending bar, as patrons sometimes got a little too comfortable, eased their way around the corner of the bar, and ended up blocking the kitchen door. On this night in 2008, Kevin noticed a silhouetted figure standing in the kitchen just beyond the doorway. He did a double-take, trying to focus on who or *what* he was seeing. It appeared to be a man approximately five feet ten inches tall, wearing a long coat and a fedora hat. Kevin rushed about seven feet to the end of the bar to ask the gentleman to move to the front of the bar, but by the time he reached the spot, the man was gone. "I was dumbfounded. I was so cognizant of that space and the need to keep it clear. Yet I couldn't find the guy I just saw. Like I said, the bar was packed; I thought someone had to have seen him," Kevin explained. Of course, upon surveying the patrons in that immediate area, Kevin found that none of them had seen the "Fedora Man."

About a year later, one of the other bartenders, Tom Vaught, witnessed this same silhouetted figure in the same doorway. Tom

**Kevin Bohl, bartender at the Brooklyn Inn**

said the figure appeared to be leaning against the doorframe and staring out towards the bar. Just as with Kevin, once Tom reached the doorway to ask the gentleman to step away, he was gone. At first, Kevin told no one what he had seen. He was both shocked and somewhat relieved when Tom confided in him about having seen Fedora Man. They compared notes and arrived at the conclusion that they both had seen the same thing.

During my visit to the Brooklyn Inn, I took several pictures of the doorway area from both sides. Although I did not capture any apparition on my digital camera, I did notice the unsettling coolness of the air at the doorway as compared to other areas of the former kitchen and the bar. I looked behind the bar near this doorway to see if there was a refrigerator or ice machine that would account for the cooler temperature, but I saw neither. A couple of my photos do have some orbs in them, and as much as I would love to definitively call them paranormal manifestations, I simply cannot. The ban on smoking in New York City bars has reduced the number of false positives inherent in ghost photography. However, at this site there is a dust factor to consider: because the main entrance door is opened and closed so frequently, airborne particulates are bound to appear in digital pictures.

I met with Lauren Macaulay, a bartender employed at the Brooklyn Inn for over nine years. She pointed out the gorgeous hand-carved woodwork which was imported from Germany and dates back to 1870. Lauren showed me how the panels on the lower half of the wall can be removed, revealing old wallpaper behind the wooden façade. I asked Lauren if she has ever seen Fedora Man, and she said, "No." She added that on several occasions she has felt uncomfortable, as if she were being observed by some ghostly presence. This feeling had come over her on occasions when the bar was busy and also when it was quiet.

Kevin confirmed that he had experienced a similar feeling, but only after hours. He described how he would close the bar at 4 A.M., then curl up in the corner with a book and a beer, hoping to unwind a bit before heading home. Instead, he would be overcome with an unnerving feeling. Rather than relaxing and winding down from his shift, he became anxious. The feeling would become unbearable, and he would lock up and leave for the night.

I inspected the basement of the Brooklyn Inn and did not capture any EVP or temperature differences indicative of paranormal activity. Usually I do not like basements, but this one did not bother me. I felt more "energy" in the bar area and in the former kitchen area. I carefully reviewed all my audio recordings of my interviews to determine if any other voices chimed in with answers or thoughts. Since there was so much background noise (the bar had been open for business while I was there), I used software to visually review the recordings to document the voice paths for Kevin, Lauren, and me, as well as the overall background noise.

Lauren mentioned one other strange thing that had happened while she was tending bar. On a slow night with very few customers, she noticed at the far end of the bar a full glass of Guinness sitting on the bar and a woman's sweater on the bar stool. At first she thought nothing of it, figuring the other bartender on duty had served a customer who might now be in the ladies' room. A while later, the glass was still full and the sweater was still on the bar stool, so Lauren asked the other bartender what happened to that patron. The other bartender thought Lauren was the one who had served up the stout. By closing time, the drink and the sweater were still there. No one ever came to claim the sweater, and the bartender poured the beer down the drain. "It still bugs me to this day," Lauren said. "How did that beer get to the bar? Why was the sweater there? The place wasn't crowded at all. I can account for each person there, but not that one." At this point in our conversation, Lauren showed me her arms. Merely retelling the experience had brought out goosebumps.

Could Fedora Man be the inspector who certified the building for occupancy back in 1957? That would explain his hat and coat and his need to inspect the place. It is also interesting that he has appeared both before and after the renovation of the kitchen area. I suggest you visit the Brooklyn Inn, belly up to the bar—toward the end by the former kitchen—and have yourself a drink. Better yet, order two drinks in case the owner of the sweater returns and wants her Guinness.

# CHAPTER 3

# Ear Inn

You WOULDN'T KNOW IT TO LOOK at the place today, but the bank of the Hudson River used to be about five feet from the Ear Inn. This Federal-style townhouse was built in 1817 for James Brown, a wealthy tobacco merchant and former aide to General George Washington. Brown sold his house in 1833. Around that time, fill dirt was brought in to expand the bank out to West Street, and new, larger piers were constructed. Thomas Cloke bought the Brown House in 1890.

Seeing all the thirsty sailors and longshoremen arriving daily at the piers, Cloke and his brother started their own brewery in the basement of the house. They sold their home-brewed beer and whiskey at the docks. However, Cloke saw the writing on the wall with the Eighteenth Amendment coming, and he sold the business in 1919.

The Brown House operated as a speakeasy during Prohibition. The upstairs rooms serving as boarding flops, a brothel, and a smuggler's den. After Prohibition, the home was known as "the Green Door Saloon" to seafaring gents who came ashore for a drink. No women were allowed. In 1969, the Landmarks Preservation Commission deemed the Brown House a historic landmark, but by then the SoHo area was in a state of decline. Around 1973, two students who were renting rooms in the house decided to buy the building. They fixed it up as best they could with their meager funds. Using spray paint, they changed the old neon sign from "BAR" to "EAR," thus renaming the place The Ear Inn.

Business picked up for the two young men; among its notable guests were John Lennon and Salvador Dali. In 1977, Martin Sheridan bought the Ear Inn, and he has been running it ever since.

Martin is well aware of the ghosts in his bar and is quite comfortable with them. The "headliner" is Mickey, a sailor who once lived upstairs and was hit and killed by a car in front of the bar. While I couldn't find any obituaries to substantiate this story, I did find several ghost books that place the accident in the 1940s or 1950s. Mickey makes his presence known by giving people seated at the bar a little nudge, occasionally pinching the derrières of lady patrons. When they turn around to see who's there, no one is. Mickey has also been blamed for disappearing pints, but Martin suspects that the absentmindedness of the customer is the more likely culprit.

Martin told me that about fifteen years ago the BBC sent over a television crew to do a documentary on the Ear Inn. They investigated and stayed in the Inn for three solid days. Their psychic concluded that three or four spirits reside at the Ear Inn. She assured Martin that they were all friendly and that he is not in any danger. However, that didn't ease the minds of the family who were renting the rooms at the time. They were fearful, as well as extremely tired, due to beign awakened frequently by a violent shaking of their beds. The family moved out, and Martin didn't bother to rent the space again. Now he uses the rooms for storage, and whenever waitresses go up there for supplies, they always declare that they will not go up there again. Something up there terrifies them.

The ghost of Mickey has nudged Martin on occasion. Martin is not frightened by it; most times, he simply tells the ghost, "I'm busy. Don't bother me." As for the patrons of the bar, newcomers who "sense a presence" sometimes ask if they can go upstairs and look around, but the regulars are not fazed by the activity at all. I asked Martin if he's ever seen a full-body apparition. "No," he said, "but customers, not bar staff, have reported seeing shapes or shadows, never a complete ghost."

I asked Martin if there are any peak times for activity. Martin says he has never noticed any cyclical patterns. "It's sporadic, probably happening more than I notice. When it's quiet in the bar, between crowds, is when I'm more apt to feel something or experience something. When the bar is busy, I'm too distracted to notice," he explained.

So, is Martin ready for a team of full-blown paranormal investigators to come in and conduct a formal investigation? No. He told me: "I live in a very old house, and I came from a very old house. The spirits there were not always nice. When the psychic from the BBC told me that these spirits were friendly, I was happy with that. I don't want a team coming in here and telling me otherwise."

I admit, I wouldn't want a team of paranormal investigators to tell me that my business is infested with negative ghosts. Who would? But I think Martin is misunderstanding the paranormal investigator. Psychics are interested in ghosts' emotional state of being. Paranormal investigators are more about simply proving that a ghost is or isn't there.

As I was leaving the Ear Inn, I chatted with a customer who was waiting outside for a friend. I asked the young man if he'd ever been to the Ear Inn before. He confirmed he had, many times, and that the burgers are "awesome." I then asked him if he had ever experienced anything paranormal. Looking shocked, he said, "You mean like ghosts?" I said, "Yes—in particular, the ghost of Mickey, who was killed out front here by a car and haunts this bar now." He told me he'd never heard the ghost story before, but that now he was totally intrigued and would pay closer attention.

I agree with his plan and advise you to pay close attention when you visit the Ear Inn. Take pictures, and have a digital recorder running in your breast pocket or in an outer pocket of your purse. You might capture something. Enjoy a burger, and be ready for a nudge or a pinch from Mickey.

# CHAPTER 4

# Manhattan Bistro

LOCATED AT 129 SPRING STREET in the SoHo section
of New York City is the Manhattan Bistro. The building is the
oldest one on Spring Street. It's a restaurant that serves Franco-
American cuisine, including duck à l'orange and grilled salmon.
The day I visited, the weather was sunny and warm, and the
front window partitions had been removed so patrons could dine
in the fresh air and sunshine. I've never been one to choose the
window seat at restaurants; it makes me feel like a caged animal

at the zoo with passersby watching me eat. If you are one who loves the window seat, especially sans window, this is the spot for you. Inside the Manhattan Bistro, you'll find a cozy atmosphere and a lovely bar. Aside from wine bottles flying off the shelf or the sight of a ghostly young woman with disheveled hair and a moss-covered skirt, it's your average bistro.

"The Ghost of Spring Street" is famous for being sighted in the immediate area of the Manhattan Bistro. It's a fascinating story that begins in 1799.

Four years before Alexander Hamilton and Aaron Burr faced each other in their famous duel, they were members of a legal dream-team hired by Ezra Weeks for his brother, Levi, who had been accused of murdering Guliana Elmore Sands.

Guliana—or "Elma," as she was called—lived on Greenwich Street in a boardinghouse owned by her aunt and uncle. On the night of December 22, 1799, she was seen departing the boardinghouse in a rented sleigh with Levi Weeks and another unidentified man. Hours later, Levi returned alone. Elma's cousin Catherine Ring, who also resided at the boardinghouse, asked Levi if he knew Elma's whereabouts, but he said he had no idea and had not even seen Elma that evening. Catherine was concerned—especially because her cousin had recently confided in her that she planned to marry Levi.

About a week later, two young boys playing near a well of the Manhattan Water Company saw what they thought was a scarf floating in the well. They ran and told police, who returned and conducted a thorough investigation. The object turned out to be a muff Elma had borrowed the evening she went missing. Using special hooks, police recovered Elma's battered body from the well. On January 2, 1800, Levi was formally charged with Elma's murder.

At the trial, attorneys Burr, Hamilton, and Livingston danced around the prosecution's evidence. They brought in several witnesses to confirm Levi's alibi for the night of the murder. The defense further asserted that Elma was promiscuous and that when Levi rescinded his proposal of marriage, Elma was so devastated she killed herself.

The medical examiner testified that Elma was dead before she was tossed in the well. He described bruises on her neck that resulted from being strangled. Witnesses for the prosecution said they saw Elma in Levi's rented sleigh, and sleigh tracks found around the well. The prosecution maintained that Levi had plenty of time to murder Elma, dispose of her body in the well, and arrive at his brother's house to form his alibi.

Additionally, Levi had approached Catherine prior to the trial and had asked her to sign an affidavit stating that he had no more interest in Elma than in any other female residing at the boardinghouse, and that, on the contrary, it was well known that Levi had an established *friendship* with Elma and nothing more.

The persistent arguments of the defense attorneys dragged the trial on for hours. It should be noted that the laws of the day required court cases to be argued and deliberated with no interruptions until a verdict was reached. At one point, the jury asked the judge for a "sleep break"; the request was denied. The exhausted jury members returned a "not guilty" verdict after only thirty minutes of deliberation. According to Charles J. Adams III, author of *New York City Ghost Stories*, the verdict outraged Catherine, and she put a curse on Hamilton, Burr, and the judge by saying, "If thee dies a natural death, I shall think there is no justice in heaven!" The curse must have worked, at least in part. Hamilton died in the famous duel with Burr. Although Burr would eventually die of a stroke, the duel destroyed his reputation. The judge simply vanished some time after the trial. Levi was so tormented by people who believed he killed Elma that he moved to Natchez, Mississippi.

Years later, there were several reports on Spring Street and near Greene Street of a ghostly young woman with long brown hair and a torn dress covered in moss. Some reports say the ghost was pointing toward the well where Elma Sands' body was found.

I visited the Manhattan Bistro, which is at 129 Spring Street near Greene, and spoke with restaurant manager Thomas King. Thomas has worked at the Bistro for eleven years. Recently he participated in the filming of an episode of *Ghost Stories* for the Travel Channel. Thomas explained to me that the well where Elma Sands was found was unearthed during the excavation of the Manhattan Bistro's basement. To his knowledge no one has ever seen a mist coming from the well, as has been reported in other books and articles. Thomas said, "The well is in the basement, not open to the public's view. No one has seen that well since the 1800s except for us. It's in my office; my desk is right next to it. I've never seen any mist." I asked him if things ever go missing in his office or if he's experienced any other paranormal manifestations. He said, "One time I came down to my office, and before I turned the light on, I heard a woman's voice say, 'I'm sorry,' very distinctly. It was very freaky." On another occasion, Thomas went to the basement to retrieve bar supplies, which are kept behind a locked metal gate. He unlocked the gate, left the key in the lock, and went into the storage space. Within seconds, he had that uneasy feeling that says, "Turn around." When he did, he saw that the gate was locked and the keys were resting on a box about ten feet out of his reach. Thomas had not heard any of the noises he should have, such as the gate dragging on the floor to close or the ring of keys jingling as the gate key was turned and removed from the lock. Nor did he hear the sound of someone performing these actions and then racing up the stairs so as not to be seen. Thomas called for help, but it was an hour or so before one of the staff realized he hadn't returned from the

**Patrons enjoy drinks at the Manhattan Bistro.**

basement and came to find him locked in the storage space.

In our conversation, Thomas confirmed reports of wine bottles flying off shelves and of ashtrays levitating and smashing against walls back when smoking was permitted. I asked Thomas if perhaps the bottles fell off the shelf from the vibration of a subway train, but he said the subway is not close enough to cause such a vibration. He also told me about the exploding glasses. "I was talking on the phone, by the bar, and had my hand resting on the shelf. Suddenly, a champagne glass flew through the air and exploded. A big piece of glass cut me between my pinky and ring finger. I had to go to the emergency room to get stitches."

Thomas doesn't blame Elma's ghost for his injury; he senses her presence as a gentle spirit. Hiowever, he also senses the spirit of a man who hanged himself on the third floor of the building in the 1920s; that ghost, he says, is angry and malevolent.

According to Thomas, there are certain areas of the restaurant where paranormal phenomena happen more frequently. For instance, often when he is walking down the stairs to his basement office, not only will he feel a tugging at his shirt, he can see the fabric being pulled by an unseen hand. Bottles fly off the bar shelves. By the maitre'd stand, Thomas has had the sensation many times that his left arm is ice-cold and wet. The first time it happened, he thought a cold liquid was dripping down the length of his arm. When he touched the arm with his right hand and realized it was dry, he feared he had some kind of nerve damage. A couple of days later, he noticed one of the waiters at the maitre'd stand patting his left arm with his right hand. Thomas had never said a word to anyone about the sensation he had experienced at that spot, yet when he asked the waiter what he was doing, the waiter said he couldn't understand why his left arm had this ice-cold, wet feeling that dragged down from his shoulder to his wrist. The sensation has happened to Thomas several more times and as recently as three weeks prior to my interviewing him. He hasn't noticed a rhythm or pattern to the paranormal activity at the Manhattan Bistro. "It happens sporadically," he said.

Electrical issues abound at the restaurant even though the wiring is up to code and the establishment always passes routine fire inspections. "Two weeks ago," Thomas said, "I touched the extension cord that's plugged into the stereo, and a spark flew from it and I got a shock that went through my entire body. Everyone at the bar saw this happen. It's very strange because the extension cord is one of those heavy-duty types with a surge protector. I've also gotten shocked just turning off a light switch," Thomas explained. He's been shocked a total of six times, always in the area of the maitre'd stand or near the credenza by the stairs.

Thomas has sustained one other injury while at the Bistro. While working in the kitchen, he looked down to see his fingers being forced around the handle of a knife. He watched in horror as he involuntarily sliced halfway through the thumb of his other hand. Again, he required stitches, and he was unable to play the piano for almost a year.

With all the paranormal activity at the Manhattan Bistro, I was not surprised when Thomas told me it's the third most haunted building in New York City. I didn't get a chance to ask him what the first two are before he went into another ghost story. This one happened a few years ago to the owner's daughter, who used to work at the bistro. When she would leave at night, all the lights would shut off simultaneously. It's physically impossible for one person to do this; the switches are on several different walls, and a couple of them are dimmer switches that slide to the "off" position. Yet whenever the young woman put her hand on one switch to shut it off, all the lights in the bistro would go out before she had a chance to flip even the one switch.

Several times, late at night when no one is in the building, the water tap in the sink at the waiters' station has turned on and run full force, partially flooding the restaurant. Thomas said they have replaced the sink and faucet three times, and it still happens. He's also replaced the doorknob on the right-hand ladies' bathroom stall several times. Patrons have complained that "a force" holds the doorknob of that stall so tightly the customer cannot turn it. The lady gets so frustrated and frightened that she ends up damaging the doorknob or the hinges on the door. In this same stall, the toilet lid sometimes lowers itself silently. Women have taken time to line the seat with toilet tissue, and when they go to sit down, the lid is down.

Even though smoking is not allowed in New York City restaurants, Thomas says that quite frequently he'll smell cigarette smoke downstairs by his office. The first time it happened, he went upstairs to chastise the lawbreaker, but no one was smoking there. Thomas attributes the smoke smell to the man who hanged himself upstairs in the 1920s, whom Thomas describes as "a tortured artist."

Thomas recalled that, his first day on the job, he was downstairs in the then-manager's office, seated on a chair by the well. The manager told Thomas that she believed the restaurant was haunted, and he said he didn't believe in any of "that stuff." With that, his chair lifted from behind and pushed him forward about four feet. He hasn't doubted the ghosts since.

On many occasions when Thomas has been alone in his basement office, he's heard the sound of footsteps walking up the stairs. The footsteps continue across the restaurant (due to the terrazzo tile floor, footsteps in the restaurant are easily heard in the basement). Halfway across the room, the footsteps stop. Where Thomas hears them stop is right above the well.

Thomas concluded our interview by saying that so many little things happen daily that he can't keep track of them; he only takes notice of the significant ones. If you dine here, you might order the duck à l'orange—and you may have to actually *duck* to avoid being pelted by an errant champagne glass or wine bottle. Bon appétit!

# CHAPTER 5

# McSorley's Old Ale House

JOHN MCSORLEY ARRIVED in New York City from Liverpool in 1851 on the ship *Colonist*. In 1854 he opened a saloon at 15 East Seventh Street, naming it The Old House at Home. It was a place for Irish immigrant workingmen to come and feel at home as they enjoyed a beer with some cheese and crackers. By 1908 a storm had ripped the original sign down, and it was replaced with a new sign bearing a new name: McSorley's Old Time Ale House. Later on, the word *Time* was removed from the name, and to this day the establishment is called McSorley's Old Ale House.

In 1910, at the age of 83, John McSorley died in his apartment above the bar. His son Bill took over the business. By 1936, two years before his death, Bill sold the bar to its first non-McSorley owner, Daniel O'Connell. Only a year later, in 1939, O'Connell died, leaving the bar to his daughter, Dorothy O'Connell Kirwan. Dorothy promised her father she would not allow women in the bar, and she kept that promise. She appointed her husband, Harry Kirwan, as the manager. Dorothy entered the bar only on Sundays, after closing time. Eventually, ownership was passed along to the Kirwans' son, Danny.

The next owner of McSorley's was Matthew Maher. He and Harry Kirwin had met by chance when Harry was visiting Ireland in 1964. Harry's car broke down, and along came Matthew Maher to save the day. In return, Harry promised Maher a job if he ever came to New York City. Later that year, Matthew Maher began his employment at McSorley's as a waiter and bartender. Maher was promoted to night manager of the bar, and in 1977 he purchased the bar from Danny Kirwan.

McSorley's has been the subject of a stage play, of poetry by e.e. cummings, and of artwork by John Sloan. Its list of notable guests ranges from Abraham Lincoln to Woody Guthrie and John Lennon. The very chair Lincoln sat in is up above the bar, in fact; a few feet away hangs one of the original "Wanted" posters for John Wilkes Booth. Amazingly, the first time women were allowed in McSorley's was in 1969, following a lawsuit, although a ladies' restroom was not installed until 1990. Today, McSorley's is the fourth oldest bar in New York City. (The oldest is the Bridge Café, another entry in this book; it is believed to have opened in 1794.)

My mother and I visited McSorley's Ale House in January 2010. The bar is within walking distance of Cooper University, which I am sure the students there greatly appreciate. The swinging wooden doors with their oval windows are worn along the edges from 156 years of use. Sawdust is strewn over the floor, and a coal-burning potbellied stove keeps the place warm and inviting.

I met with a bartender known as Pepe who has bartended at McSorley's since 1973. At first I thought it odd to see a black plastic garbage bag suspended at his waist under his apron, but I soon realized how much sense it made as waterproofing, or beer-proofing, for his trousers. Pepe's real name is Steven Zwaryczuk. He's not fazed by the reports of ghosts and other paranormal activity at McSorley's. In fact, he laughingly pointed out two reg-ular customers, Brian and Mark, as the most paranormal things to happen to him. Brian has been coming to McSorley's since the early 1980s, when he was in the eighth grade. Back then, he said, he was the same height as he is now and weighed only about twenty pounds less. Mark was at the end of the bar where Mini, the cat, was curled up in the corner. I asked Pepe, "Has there been any time when you were completely 'creeped out' by being here?" Without missing a beat, he pointed to Brian and replied: "Nothing has ever creeped me out except him!"

Mark chimed in that a friend of his who once rented the apartment above the bar would occasionally hear tables and chairs moving, as well as distant voices, long after the bar was closed for the night.

Pepe was kind enough to bring owner Matthew Maher down to the bar so I could interview him. Although Matthew has been living and working in New York City since 1964, he's maintained a sweet Irish brogue. I asked him, "Have you had any ghostly experiences while working here?" and he chuckled and said, "Have ya got a year to spare?" Well, that certainly got my attention.

Maher told me that McSorley's is famous for always having at least one feline "on staff" at the bar. One night after closing, Maher was cleaning the kitchen. He returned to the bar area and saw the cat at the end of the bar purring and nuzzling up against an unseen hand that was petting it. According to Dr. Philip Ernest Schoenberg, tour guide for Ghosts of New York,

**Minnie is part of a long tradition of cats at McSorley's.**

whenever a cat is seen in the window of McSorley's, Harry Houdini is present as the spirit inside the cat. Why Houdini, you ask? Dr. Schoenberg claims that the set of handcuffs secured to the footrail of the bar once belonged to Houdini.

Maher also pointed out the print depicting McSorley's that hangs behind the bar. He said that when a local artist presented the print to him, Maher immediately commented, "Very nice! You even included one of the McSorley's cats." The artist, appearing confused, stood back and carefully examined the print. He told Maher that he never painted the cat and had no idea how it ended up in the finished print. The cat's body is facing the entrance of McSorley's, but its head is turned, looking over its shoulder toward the rear of the dining area.

According to Ted Andrews in his book *Animal Speak,* cats represent mystery, magic, independence, and nighttime. In ancient Egypt, the cat was revered and usually represented the goddess Bast. Cats have been associated with witches as their "familiars." In this respect, it is believed that the cat embodies the spirit of a former witch who crossed the line and did something worthy of punishment. That punishment is to incarnate as a cat and serve the needs of another witch for nine lives before being allowed to incarnate once more as a human. It's interesting to note that cats are typically feminine in their energies and connections. McSorley's did not allow women in the bar until 1970, yet the cats have been present all along.

Brian pointed out to me a dust-covered gas lamp that hangs in McSorley's. On it are several turkey wishbones, also covered with dust. McSorley's tradition calls for a soldier leaving for war to place a wishbone on the lamp, then remove it when he returns. Brian thinks this tradition started with World War I; other sources claim it started with the Civil War. Other than a soldier leaving or reclaiming his wishbone, no one is allowed to touch the gas lamp, not even to clean it. Brian said that the dusty wishbones still on the lamp serve as a memorial of sorts for the soldiers who placed them there before leaving for war and never returned.

I doubt Houdini is hanging around McSorley's as a cat. However, the disembodied noises, the unseen admirer seen petting the cat on the bar, and the lengthy history of notable guests at the establishment certainly lend credence to assertions that the place is haunted. Personally, I did not capture any evidence of paranormal happenings. Rather, my mother and I were captured by the mouthwatering aroma of the burgers that landed on the table by the front window for a young couple having lunch. The motto of McSorley's is "Be Good or Be Gone." Apparently, someone is being good for an indefinite amount of time, as they're not yet gone. Keep this in mind if you visit McSorley's, and order an extra round of "light & dark" beer when you belly up to the bar.

# CHAPTER 6

# Old Bermuda Inn

THE OLD BERMUDA INN is a sprawling banquet facility
with a twist. Embedded within it is the original structure of a
single-family home built in 1832. The home is now the Inn's
restaurant, and across the parking lot is a quaint outbuilding
that serves as a bed-and-breakfast. For customers ranging from
discriminating brides to planners of lavish company holiday
parties, the Old Bermuda Inn fits the bill with its ambiance and
fine-quality food.

The Mesereaus were the first couple to live in the home and
enjoy the view of the New York harbor. Young Martha Mesereau
looked forward to starting a family, but the Civil War interrupted
her plans. Her husband was drafted to serve in the Union forces
and, sadly, was killed in action. Martha was grief-stricken. She

The portrait of Martha Mesereau, marred by a burn mark from a mysterious fire

retreated to the small bedroom, locked the door, and starved herself to death.

Today, Martha's presence is experienced as a distinct and chilling cold spot and by the sounds of someone moving around on the second floor when no one is there. Managers at the restaurant have investigated the sounds of a woman weeping on the second floor but have found no one. Often, there are reports of a phantom-like lady roaming the dining rooms or appearing on the staircase, and her description matches the portrait of Martha that hangs at the entrance of the restaurant, opposite the staircase.

In addition to cold spots, Martha has a thing for heat, as in fire. In each of the six fireplaces, fires have started mysteriously. During a renovation, the portrait of Martha self-ignited; luckily, the fire was contained immediately, and the portrait remains intact save for a few scorch marks. The staff are convinced that Martha was not pleased by the renovations.

The day my son Brian and I went to investigate the Old Bermuda Inn was Martin Luther King, Jr. day. I called ahead to make sure they were open, given that it was a Monday and a holiday. The receptionist said, "We're open seven days a week." The traffic gods were on my side as I approached the Outerbridge Crossing (a bridge) with absolutely no one in my way. For those of you unfamiliar with the area, traffic is customarily backed up to Route 287, forcing one to inch all the way down to 440 and over the bridge.

Once inside, the receptionist greeted us and explained that Cindy, the general manager, had left instructions to expect us and to convey her apologies that she could not be there. The receptionist handed us a flyer about the inn's history that details some of the haunted activity there. Then she said, "Follow me." Walking through the dining room, she pointed to the chandelier and told us, "People say they see one of the lights glowing when the chandelier is turned off." (According to the flyer, "Martha is keeping a light on while she waits for her long lost love.") Next, she took us to the portrait of Martha Mesereau. Pointing out the burn mark, she told us how the portrait caught fire during renovations when nothing nearby could have burned it.

Brian and I were left to wander the dining areas, the bar, and the second floor. We were on our own except for a catering manager and his two clients who walked by once as we stood in the downstairs hallway. There was activity in the kitchen, but nothing paranormal; the cooks were cleaning and prepping. We took several pictures of Martha's portrait from various angles and positions. I left my digital voice recorder on the table in front of her portrait to record possible EVPs while we toured the adjoining rooms on the first floor. The average temperature in each room was approximately sixty-eight degrees. I retrieved the recorder before heading up to the second floor.

Upstairs, Brian and I had the whole floor to ourselves. This was perfect. It was quiet. The door of one room was slightly ajar; I peeked inside and saw chairs, tables, catering equipment, appointment books, and a bride's hoop skirt and tulle. I thought it odd that this storage room was left unlocked. Later in my research, I read about the former bedroom that baffles the Inn's staff because they find its door open when they know for sure that they locked it the night before. It's thought that this is the room where Martha died.

In the larger room just beyond the unlocked storage room, Brian got out his camera to take pictures. At first he saw nothing out of the ordinary, but then his camera had an odd malfunction. Actually, it would have been functioning perfectly if someone had been in front of the lens. However, when he took a picture in the outer corner of the room, the camera went into face-focus mode, attempting to center and focus on a person's face even though there was no one there that Brian could see. He thought something was wrong with his camera, but when he pointed it at the other corners of the room, it took pictures successfully without attempting to focus on a face.

Brian found me in the hallway outside the bathrooms and told me what had just happened with his camera. I followed him back to that room and took pictures with my camera. I had no problems, but my camera is a less advanced Nikon than Brian's. He took some more pictures and the camera worked fine until he pointed it to the corner of the room where it had malfunctioned before. Again, the camera searched as if trying to focus on a face. This time I was there to witness it.

In the view screen on the back of the camera, I saw a blurry shape in the corner of the room. Whatever it was, the camera wanted to focus on it before it would allow the shot to be taken; I could hear the lens shifting in and out. Finally the camera just shut off, as if it were exhausted from focusing and had given up.

I asked Brian if he had shut the camera off. Looking rather perplexed, he said no. It's unlikely that he shut it off acciden-

**The beautiful chandelier at the haunted Old Bermuda Inn**

tally. The power button on his camera has to be pressed and held down to turn the camera off; this prevents the user from accidentally powering down while taking a picture.

As we left the room quickly, I asked Brian, "Is the battery drained?"

We stopped at the top of the main staircase. Brian pushed the power button, and the camera powered on perfectly. The battery level indicator read 90 percent, and the camera functioned properly as Brian took his last few pictures on the first floor and outside the building.

Martha's ghost didn't leave any EVPs on my audio recorder, but I think she liked having her picture taken by a young man. It's possible that she was there in that room and saw my son not as a stranger but as her dearly departed husband. Ghosts have a tendency to see people and places as they remember them, not as they are; it's part of their confused state of being. Given how tragically Martha took the news of her husband's death, it's a safe bet that her earthbound spirit is quite confused.

I found a Web site where ghosthunters and paranormal enthusiasts post their findings and thoughts about various locations that may or may not be haunted. Those who have posted comments about the Old Bermuda Inn range from believers to doubters to those who say it's not haunted at all. If you're bored—and if you do not suffer stomach upset from occasional exposure to gross misspellings, poor grammar, and completely erroneous information—you can review the site for yourself; the link is in the Directory of Places at the end of this book. I suspect the Old Bermuda Inn has more going on than just its advertised dinner and dancing specials. Make a reservation; Martha's waiting for you.

CHAPTER 7

# One If By Land, Two If By Sea

THIS RESTAURANT IS TOUTED as one of the most romantic in New York City. It opened in 1972 as a business partnership between Mario DeMartini and Armand Braiger. Many men have "popped the question" here. I personally haven't eaten here, as the food appears to be more of a work of art on a plate than something edible. You know the type: it's all about presentation, and then after dinner, you head to the nearest drive-through to actually eat. They get rave reviews for their artsy food, so please don't think I'm putting it down. I'm just a gal who likes—okay, loves—to eat, so I need food on my plate, not a sculpture. I can, however, give this restaurant a "thumbs up" for the romantic ambiance, as I'm a sucker for candlelit dinners.

If you're visiting this restaurant specifically for its ghostly aspect, I suggest you sit at the bar, enjoy the piano music, and be very careful walking downstairs to the restrooms. The ghost here is known to push people down the stairs. Since I tend to be gravity-challenged on occasion, I was especially careful to hold the railing when I made my way to the ladies' room during my visit.

There is a lot of history that factors into the possible identities of the spirits here. First of all, this structure was originally the carriage house of the Richmond Hill estate of Aaron Burr, and it was located at Spring Street and Sixth Avenue, about three blocks up from what today is the entrance to the Holland Tunnel. The estate was acquired by John Jacob Astor after Burr's 1807 trial for his July 11, 1804, duel with Alexander Hamilton. Astor moved the mansion fifty-five feet downhill to what is now the corner of Varick and Charlton Streets, and he moved the livery stable to 106 West Third Street. The carriage house, now the subject of our investigation, was moved to 17 Barrow Street. From the 1950s to 1984, the livery stable was a coffee house called Café Bizarre; sightings of a stern-faced Burr were reported there. New York University eventually took over the property for dormitory space, so the carriage house became Burr's final haunt.

When Aaron Burr lived at Richmond Hill with his wife and two daughters, it was *the* place to dine and be entertained. Burr served the best wine at his lavish dinners, and his teen-age daughter, Theodosia, played hostess, as her mother was too ill. Once Burr's wife died, Theodosia became his confidant and companion. In fact, it was a snide comment about Burr's supposedly having an incestuous relationship with his daughter, uttered by Alexander Hamilton at a social event, that led to the fateful duel.

Theodosia married Joseph Alston and moved to his plantation in South Carolina in 1801. They had a son whom they named Aaron Burr Alston. Theodosia suffered medical compli-

**The restaurant's romantic interior**

cations after the birth of her son and was unable to have any more children. Tragically, little Aaron died of malaria at the age of ten. To alleviate her grief, Burr invited Theodosia to visit him in New York. She accepted the invitation and boarded the *Pioneer* on December 31, 1812. When the ship did not arrive on schedule, Burr thought his daughter had perished at sea. One legend tells that a pirate was later captured and that some of Theodosia's jewelry was found in his possession. Supposedly he confessed to pirating the *Pioneer* and forcing those on board, including Theodosia in her flowing white gown, to walk the plank to their deaths. In other versions of the legend, the ship was called *Patriot* and was simply lost at sea.

After Theodosia's disappearance and presumed death, Burr had all her belongings packed and stored in the basement of his carriage house. That would explain the attachment of his and

Theodosia's spirits to the place. On rare occasions, full-body apparitions have been sighted at the restaurant—usually late at night, after closing. Aaron Burr has been seen by employees, as well as a lady in a long white gown who descends the stairs and vanishes. They describe the gown as having an empire waist, a style that was fashionable in 1812, when Theodosia was lost at sea.

Another ghost spotted at One If By Land, Two If By Sea is that of an African-American man who is seen upstairs seated at a small table. By the time the waiter arrives to take his order, the mysterious guest has vanished. He has not been identified, but some suspect he is Burr's devoted manservant of thirty years. I wonder if he could be James Brown, a tobacco merchant whose house was built in 1817 at the base of the Richmond Hill estate. Today, that home is the Ear Inn at 326 Spring Street, another haunted spot in this book.

Over the years, One If By Land, Two If By Sea has had consistent poltergeist activity, mainly harmless pranks. Napkins have been pulled off customers' laps; chairs have moved as the customer attempts to sit down. Unseen hands move salt and pepper shakers. This telekinetic energy or poltergeist activity is strong enough to push an adult down the stairs. Two electricians working here witnessed their tools levitating and floating toward them; they were so frightened that they ran out and refused to return, not even to collect their fee.

The establishment is haunted by typical residual sounds, such as glasses clinking and heavy footsteps pounding across the third floor above the manager's office when no one is there. More baffling is the sound of a cat meowing, as animals are not allowed in the restaurant. The sounds also include human voices; a customer or employee will hear someone calling his name from behind, and when he turns around, no one is there. Once the office copier started itself and began spewing out blank pages, which frightened one skeptical employee into believing "there are such things as ghosts."

When I arrived at One If By Land, Two If By Sea, the head waiter and manager, Andreas, was quick to invite me in. He showed me around briefly, pointing out that the brick inside the bar is original, although the bar itself is new. Andreas also told me that two tombs had been discovered during excavation in the basement, but he was too pressed for time to take me down there. He was in a rush to get to the store to purchase some replacement light bulbs. As he dashed out the door, he said, "Feel free to walk anywhere you want."

I went first to the staircase that leads to the balcony dining room; this is where the ghost lady is seen coming down the stairs. It was a great vantage point for capturing pictures of the restaurant and bar below. I didn't document any temperature drops, and no one pushed me—thankfully, as both my hands were occupied with my audio recorder and camera. I called out to Theodosia and to "Vice President Burr," but upon reviewing the recordings, I heard no answers. From the balcony, I went into the main dining area. I kept the audio recorder going, and I alternated between temperature scans and picture-taking. The temperature was averaging 68 degrees. The photos showed no anomalies. Then I went into the front parlor dining rooms. These adjoining rooms are smaller and more intimate than the main dining area, and each has a beautiful fireplace. It was a few degrees warmer in these rooms, perhaps because they're smaller.

I went down the narrow staircase to the restrooms in the basement. Again I was thankful that the ghost didn't push me. I was hoping to find an entry to where the tombs had been unearthed, but the "Employees Only" door was locked. Inside the ladies' room, the heat was intense: 78 degrees! But this wasn't paranormal; I saw the radiator and realized the door had not been opened for a while, so the heat had built up.

I know a temperature drop is a more typical indication of a ghost's presence than a temperature increase. Occasionally, though, a ghost will drive the temperature up to an uncomfortable level in order to be noticed or to drive living persons away. So I kept my audio recorder going while in the stifling-hot bathroom. I did not capture any EVPs. As for the tombs, I learned that of the two headstones that were unearthed in the basement, only one was legible, and the name on it was Elizabeth Seaman. Is it possible that Elizabeth haunts the restaurant, rather than Theodosia?

Who *was* Elizabeth Seaman, I wondered? I discovered that a woman named Elizabeth Cochrane Seaman was an investigative journalist known publicly as *Nellie Bly*. The New York Press Club dedicated a headstone to her at the Woodlawn Cemetery in 1978. I asked them if there was a correlation to the headstone found at the 17 Barrow Street restaurant. They said they had no knowledge of another tomb or headstone being discovered. So the Elizabeth Seaman whose tomb was found downstairs at the restaurant is obviously not the famous one known as Nellie Bly.

"One if by land, two if by sea," as everyone knows, was the lantern signal sent to Paul Revere from the Old North Church in Boston during the Revolutionary War. Perhaps the ghosts of the restaurant play off this theme, moving one object at a diner's place setting to signal an order of beef, two objects for an order of seafood. I suppose if two objects are moved and the diner is pushed down the stairs, it means she ordered the surf and turf.

# CHAPTER 8

# White Horse Tavern

THE WHITE HORSE TAVERN is a popular destination for tourists primarily because of its association with Bohemian literary greats such as Jack Kerouac, Norman Mailer, and Dylan Thomas. The structure that houses the tavern was built in 1817 as a livery and stable; in 1880, it became a bar for sailors and longshoremen.

Fast-forward to 1950, when Welsh poet Dylan Thomas arrived in America to present a series of lectures. He was quickly introduced to the White Horse Tavern by fellow poet Ruthven Todd. Thomas favored a table by the window. He would reposition it so that it aligned perfectly with his paper while writing his poetry. When he wasn't writing at his favorite table, he was at the end of the bar hoisting another whiskey to his lips. One day in

November 1953, he had one too many. Reports vary from seventeen to nineteen shots of whiskey; suffice it to say, it was a lethal amount. After setting down his empty shot glass, he declared his consumption record-setting and proceeded to stumble out of the White Horse Tavern. He made it to his residence at the Chelsea Hotel, then collapsed. He was taken to St. Vincent's Hospital, where died of liver failure at the age of thirty-nine.

The spirit of Dylan Thomas has been witnessed at the White Horse Tavern many times. It's quite possible that the reason he lingers is that he was too drunk at the time of his death to recognize that he had died. At least twice a month, the staff find Thomas' favorite table rotated to the position he preferred, instead of where they positioned it the night before at closing.

I spoke with Rosamond Kiefer, a history major and member of the Valley Forge Historical Society, who once saw the ghost of Dylan Thomas. In June of 2002, she and two friends were touring the Museum of Natural History and then decided to walk around the East Village. By late afternoon, one of the friends who knew how much Rosamond is intrigued by the paranormal said, "Oh, you'll love this place! They say this tavern is haunted." They entered the White Horse Tavern and went to the left to sit at a table facing the long bar. The bar was not crowded at all.

Rosamond asked her friend, "Where are we supposed to see a ghost?" The friend, who had no interest whatsoever in the paranormal, had no idea. So Rosamond sat with her back to the wall to have a clear vantage point of the length of the bar, and her two friends sat across from her, facing the wall. Rosamond kept an eye on the bar as the three friends conversed. At the far end of the bar on the right-hand side, she noticed a man standing with his foot on the bar railing, his right arm raised with a glass in his hand. She heard him say, "Drinks for everyone!" No one around the man reacted—not even the bartender, who would have made quite a tip.

Seeing that no one had paid attention to the man, Rosamond figured that perhaps he had no money, and that the people around him knew that and therefore ignored him. As she stared at him, she realized his attire was not of this time period. She interrupted her friends and asked them to look at the man and give their assessments. They turned around and looked in the direction she pointed, but he was gone. Rosamond was completely baffled. How could he have left the bar so quickly? That's when it hit her: She'd seen a ghost!

At the end of that summer, Rosamond was in a bookstore and saw the book *Discovery Travel Adventure Haunted Holidays.* As she flipped through it, she found the section for New York City and saw the White Horse Tavern. She read the part about Dylan Thomas frequenting this bar when he was alive and hoisting his glass. The chill that shot up Rosamond's spine confirmed the identity of the ghost she had seen in June.

During my visit to the tavern, I took some pictures and attempted to record EVPs. I also spoke with the bartender about the haunting of the tavern. He said he had worked at the tavern for a little over two years, and that every year around Halloween, reporters come in to interview staff about the haunting. He told me he has not experienced anything paranormal and assured me that he has been there well past closing. He was intrigued when I told him about the apparition that Rosamond witnessed. I'm sure he'll be telling that story this October to the reporters that show up.

My audio recordings and photos collected nothing substantial. I can't drink alcoholic beverages when I am investigating and interviewing, so I did not hang around too long in the bars I visited for this book. Another time, I will revisit the White Horse Tavern to have a leisurely drink or two. Hopefully Dylan will join me.

# Churches

# CHAPTER 9

# St. Mark's in-the-Bowery

THE WORD *BOWERY* comes from the Dutch *bouwerie,* meaning farm. That's exactly what this place was when Petrus Stuyvesant was lord and master of the land and first governor of New Amsterdam, now known as New York. Stuyvesant arrived in the New World in 1647. Having lost a leg while fighting for the Dutch in Curacao, he had a wooden leg complete with silver studs, which earned him the nicknames "Peg Leg Peter" and "Old Silver Nails." Stuyvesant used a cane for stability, which gave his walking gait a distinct sound. While he was not known as the kindest man, he did maintain order and contribute to the development of this area of Manhattan. He had a small chapel built on his estate, and in 1672 he died and was buried in the family crypt beneath the chapel. Eventually that chapel was torn down, and on May 9, 1799, a new church was completed and dedicated on the same site. St. Mark's is the second oldest church in New York City (the oldest is St. Paul's, which also has a chapter in this book).

Petrus Stuyvesant's spirit didn't rest too long in the family crypt. Within days of his death, servants reported seeing a specter roaming the property. They concluded it was Petrus because they heard the tapping of his cane and his wooden leg. Several stories of sightings have come down to us; the stories are set in different time periods yet have common elements. The first version of the story takes place during the Civil War. A church sexton encountered the ghost of Petrus and was so frightened he ran screaming into the street, but drowning out his screams were the peals of the bell in St. Mark's tower. When a few brave men went into the church to see who had rung the bell, they found no one there—and the rope had been torn off too high for any human to reach and pull. The next day, they found the other piece of the bellrope on Petrus' grave. In another version of the story, the events are essentially the same but transpired during the 1960s, according to an article in the November 17, 2004, *New York Sun* newspaper.

Yet another variation of the story is linked to the fire that nearly destroyed St. Mark's in 1978. In this telling, it is not a sexton who encounters Petrus' ghost, but firefighters. The fire department arrived on the scene to hear St. Mark's bell ringing incessantly. Once they got inside to see who had rung the bell, no one was there, and the rope appeared to have been burned off too high for anyone to reach. Later, as the story goes, the missing length of rope was found on Petrus' grave. That last detail, the discovery of the rope on Petrus' grave, is consistent in all three tellings.

The Stuyvesant mansion was destroyed by fire in 1774, yielding reports of Petrus' ghost hobbling through the rubble and shaking his head in dismay over the loss of his home. The 1978 fire at the church collapsed the structure's roof and destroyed nine of the twenty-three stained-glass windows, but that time, no phantom Petrus was seen rummaging through the ruins.

In the 1800s, many eyewitness accounts describe Petrus' spirit roaming up and down the street by the church. People also heard his distinctive walk inside the church. In addition to Petrus' marching about the church and its grounds, a ghoulish event took place at St. Mark's in 1878. Grave robbers broke into a crypt and stole the remains of A.T. Stewart, a former entrepreneur who had made a fortune running department stores. Initially, the grave-robbers demanded a ransom of $250,000 for the remains. Stewart was notable for being the first merchant to affix price stickers on items to avoid haggling; it is especially ironic, therefore, that Mrs. Stewart haggled with the robbers over the ransom amount. for two years, eventually recovering her husband's remains for a mere $20,000. A.T. Stewart was finally laid to rest in a vault at the Cathedral of the Incarnation in Garden City, Long Island. The robbers who had defiled his crypt at St. Mark's were never apprehended.

Apparitions of Petrus seemed to end when the last of his descendants was interred in the family crypt. Yet in 1995, just before Christmas, a woman walking near St. Mark's reported hearing "a soft shuffle and then a distinct thump ... it was echoey ... like something out of an old pirate movie—some pirate shuffling along with a wooden leg." Later the woman learned about

The monument to
Petrus Stuyvesant,
who remains a
restless spirit

the haunted history surrounding the former governor and realized it was probably him she had heard "walking" behind her
that day in 1995. On another occasion, the same unidentified
woman again heard the sound of Petrus near the church; this
time, she followed it to investigate. She caught a glimpse of him
out of the corner of her eye; he was moving quickly, but with the
distinctive pacing of the wooden leg and cane.

Other ghostly sightings at St. Mark's include two female
spirits. One appears during the service near the center aisle of
the nave; just as mysteriously as she appears, she vanishes at the
conclusion of the service. The other female spirit is seen near
the organ in the balcony and by the rear entrance of the church.
Matilda Hoffman is the rumored identity of one of these spirits.

The beloved of American author Washington Irving, she died when she was seventeen years old.

The day I visited St. Mark's, many people were bustling about preparing for a musical performance. Since I didn't have a ticket, I couldn't stay long; I was allowed barely enough time to take some photos and attempt EVP recording. With performers waiting in the alcoves, technicians hoisting lighting fixtures, and others positioning chairs for the audience, the noise level was not conducive to collecting EVPs. My photos captured only the expected dust orbs.

Before leaving, I stopped at the registration table in the foyer to chat with the ladies there. I inquired as to whether they had ever encountered the ghost of Petrus or possibly seen the female spirits. The ladies were receptive to my inquiry and expressed fascination with the paranormal, but they said they hadn't witnessed any such phenomena.

I departed and found the plaque outside the church that marks the spot where Petrus Stuyvesant is interred. I listened carefully for the tapping of his wooden leg, which many have reported hearing over the years. I knelt down close to the plaque with my digital audio recorder in my hand. Unfortunately, I didn't collect any EVPs, but I did sense an "energy" emanating from the spot. For a moment, I had the sensation that if I looked up, the stern face of Petrus would be there, staring down at me. I mustered the nerve to look up and take a picture, but I saw no one and found nothing in my photo. It was just a feeling I'd had. Given the many reports of encounters, inexplicably tolling bells, and disembodied sounds, I'd say St. Mark's in-the-Bowery qualifies as a haunted site. It's rumored that your chances of glimpsing "Peg-Leg Peter" are better if you're at the church at midnight on Christmas. Perhaps then, the tapping of Petrus' wooden leg makes for a "Not-So-Silent Night."

# CHAPTER 10

# St. Paul's Chapel

PART OF TRINITY PARISH, St. Paul's Chapel is Manhattan's oldest public building; it has been in continuous operation since 1766. The chapel's place in history is marked with a pew in which General George Washington prayed before being inaugurated in 1789. Also, since the church is located directly across from the site of the former World Trade Center, it was a place of respite for emergency workers after the 9/11 disaster, offering them a place to rest and meals to replenish their strength. St. Paul's aided the rescue and recovery workers for eight months before it reverted back to its regular services. Several memorials inside the church honor those who died and those who aided on September 11, 2001.

The traumatic energies from 9/11 linger in and around St. Paul's Chapel. However, long before that tragic date, another tragic figure presented itself here: an Englishman named George Frederick Cooke. Cooke was a Shakespearean actor who came to America in 1810 to save what was left of his acting career—which had suffered immensely from his drinking problem. Initially, Cooke did well and audiences loved him, but the rebound was short-lived. He soon resumed drinking and was known for fumbling his lines and even for missing curtain calls at times.

Of course, drinking and making mistakes on stage are hardly reasons to lose one's head, but that's exactly what Cooke did. To alleviate his financial burdens, he made an agreement with his physician, Dr. John Francis, to donate his head post mortem for dissection and experimentation. When Cooke died in 1812, his head was removed per the agreement. However, instead of being sent straight to the laboratory, Cooke's skull was returned to the limelight as a stage prop in *Hamlet* (during the famous scene in which Hamlet says, "Alas, poor Yorick. I knew him . . .").

Apparently Cooke's spirit was not happy about its former head being reduced to a prop, given the commanding performances the whole actor had once given, for it was around this time that a headless, shadowy figure began to appear in the graveyard of St. Paul's Chapel. Witnesses suspected it was the ghost of Cooke searching for his head. Eventually, the skull arrived at its intended destination, the Jefferson Medical School in Philadelphia, Pennsylvania. Yet sightings of the headless ghost continue at St. Paul's, no doubt because Cooke's headless body lies there under the impressive monument marking his grave.

My visit to St Paul's was during the daytime, so I did not have the opportunity to scan for the headless ghost of George Frederick Cooke. I did walk through the graveyard, and I took some pictures. It's amazing to look out over what was once the site of the World Trade Center towers and see only a fenced crater. I walked

**The interior of St. Paul's Chapel**

to the side of the church and sat on a bench, careful to note on my audio recorder that the creaking sound on the recording was from the bench. I recorded for a few minutes while seated there, but the noise from an airplane passing overhead, people walking by, and jingling dog tags on passing pooches made it fruitless to attempt EVP work.

Inside the church, I perused the various photos and displays set up as memorials to the victims of the 9/11 tragedy. I took some pictures of the ornate altar and pulpit. I noticed that each column had a box of tissues strategically balanced on the shelf-like cap of its pedestal. I continued reviewing the memorials, making my way toward the rear of the chapel. That's when I saw the huge commemorative banner suspended across the choir loft. I don't know why, but that affected me, and my eyes began to well up with tears. I knew then why those tissue boxes were so readily available. I grabbed a tissue to dab my eyes, but, remaining in investigator mode, I snapped a picture of the banner. Instantly I saw several orbs in the image on the camera's LCD screen. I quickly took another picture, which also had orbs but not as many as the previous one. Then I realized the tissue I was using probably emitted a ton of particulates. So I waved the tissue back and forth a few times, then took another picture. Sure enough, there were a ton of orbs in that photo.

While I'm on the subject of picture-taking: Another ghost that has been seen walking past St. Paul's Chapel is that of Matthew Brady, the famous photographer who documented the Civil War and took portraits of Abraham Lincoln. Witnesses have also reported hearing the sound of Brady's walking stick near the chapel. Although his collection of photographs is priceless to us today, Brady was broke at the time of his death. Given that he had four photography studios within walking distance of St. Paul's, it's plausible that his spirit is intent on making back the money he lost toting cameras and assistants with him as he photographed the Civil War. If Brady's ghost approaches you outside St. Paul's and asks to take your picture, kindly oblige—and request that you be allowed to take one of him in return.

# CHAPTER 11

# Trinity Episcopal Church and Graveyard

TRINITY EPISCOPAL CHURCH dates back to 1696, when the petition for land to form the church was presented to Governor Benjamin Fletcher. In 1709, Trinity added a school which is now the oldest school in continuous operation in New York. The neo-gothic structure visitors see today was built in 1846; two previous buildings built on the same site were destroyed by fire or snowstorms. In 1842, seeing the need for more burial space, Trinity purchased twenty-three acres of land near John Audubon's property. The first burial at this cemetery, located at 155th and Riverside Drive, was in 1843. Trinity evolved and progressed along with the changing times. It was the first church to broadcast a radio program in 1922, and today it utilizes technology via webcasts and podcasts.

I first visited Trinity in 1986, when I worked downtown in the Merrill Lynch building. After acclimating to my new job, I ventured out at lunchtime to get acquainted with the area. I was comfortable making my way to Trinity by myself. The first time I entered its graveyard, however, was for the purpose of self-preservation. I had started out on a lunchtime stroll. A man was walking behind me. He seemed strange, but I dismissed it at first, figuring, "It's New York; there's all kinds here." I continued walking, but the uneasy feeling inside me grew. In a store window, I caught a glimpse of him and saw that he had gotten much closer to me than before. I paused for a moment, pretending to admire something in the next window, and I could see that he paused as well. I resumed walking, and so did he. My heart was beating faster and faster, and my internal warning system was sending up huge flares that said: Get to safety! I saw the entrance to the graveyard at Trinity and went in. I wandered the paths and pretended to marvel at the old gravestones, all the while keeping the man in my peripheral vision. When I saw that I could make a break for the inside of the church, that's exactly what I did. A service was in progress, so I maintained reverence despite my abrupt entrance, sat in a pew, and waited for my heart to return to a normal rhythm. When the service was over, I was able to exit with a crowd, and I made it back to the office safely. Thankfully, my boss was in a meeting and was none the wiser as to how long a lunch I had taken.

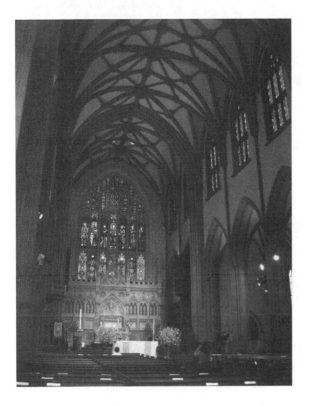

The interior of
Trinity Episcopal
Church

It was nice to get back to Trinity's graveyard on a sunny, warm spring day in 2009. I had no uneasy feeling this time, and I was able to enjoy tulips in bloom and take pictures of the gravestones. Since this graveyard is in the noisy heart of the financial district, it's not a peaceful, tranquil resting place like most cemeteries; therefore, I didn't bother trying to collect EVPs.

I turned on my digital audio recorder once I was inside the church. A tour was in progress, so I waited for the group to exit the chapel before I went in. I had the recorder balanced in my purse so it could pick up voices but not be obvious or disrespectful. Picture taking inside Trinity Church is allowed as long as a service is not in progress. The gothic design and stained glass windows contribute to beautiful photographic results. I made my way from the chapel into the church and wandered past the tour group. I took a picture from the rear of the church facing towards the altar to capture the gorgeous stained glass window. In this picture appear two orbs: one green and one white. Granted, most orbs are determined to be airborne particulates, but these two caught my attention the moment I saw the photo on my camera's LCD screen. I remained in the same spot and took several more pictures to compare the results. No other orbs appeared. In fact, this was the only picture that yielded such a result the entire time I was inside Trinity.

Next, I went to the gift shop and looked around. I wanted to speak with the sales clerk, but there were a couple people already occupying her time. So, I made my way closer to the altar by traveling up the side aisle of the church. I took pictures at various angles and intervals to see if any more "dust" would appear. Results were zero. As I made my way back to the rear of the church, I became part of the tour group, as there was no polite way to get around them without disrupting what the priest was saying. The priest was explaining about the church's organ and how the dust from the collapse of the Twin Towers on 9/11 coated the inside and outside of the organ and its pipes, rendering it useless. Trinity installed a fully digital organ in August 2003, and a free concert was performed to induct the new organ on the anniversary of September 11. The 2,000 pound digital organ is comprised of computers, software, and 150 watt to 500 watt speakers. It was supposed to be a temporary fix until another massive pipe organ could be installed in the next five years. It has been six years and Trinity is still using the digital organ.

The tour ended with a round of applause for the knowledgeable presentation and I proceeded back to the graveyard. I took a few more pictures and had to dash back to my car that was parked somewhat illegally in front of a hot dog vendor's cart. He agreed to keep an eye on it for me while I was inside the church and in exchange I purchased a couple hot dogs and chips. Granted, I can't eat the hot dogs because of certain food allergies I have, but it was still cheaper than a parking garage and very convenient.

Once home I reviewed the audio recording, and while it captured the sounds of the tour and various people milling inside the church beautifully, no EVPs were evident. The picture I have with the green orb and white orb is interesting at best, but more than likely not paranormal. Yet, I have to include Trinity Church and its graveyard as haunted sites to visit in New York City as there have been reports of seeing the ghost of Alexander Hamilton there. After his fatal duel with Aaron Burr, Hamilton was interred under an ornate obelisk monument in the graveyard. Possibly unaware of his death, he may be wondering who won the duel and, "Where's the body of Aaron?"

# Historical Sites

# CHAPTER 12

# Conference House

CONFERENCE HOUSE PARK on Staten Island spans 267 acres and includes several historic houses on site. The most notable, in terms of this book, is Conference House. Its history is impressive and its ghosts, even more so.

Let's rewind to 1674, when Captain Christopher Billopp arrived with Edmund Andros, the newly appointed royal governor of New York. In 1676, Billopp was given over 900 acres of land on the southern most point of Staten Island. He constructed his two-story home facing the Raritan Bay in 1680. The kitchen was located in the basement, and the attic provided living quarters for the servants. His property increased to 1,600 acres in 1687, and he gave it the title of "the Manor of Bentley."

Captain Billopp was a distinguished Royal Naval officer and an accomplished business man. By 1700, he owned and operated a ferry service to cross the Arthur Kill to Perth Amboy, New Jersey. He was known to be ruthless, stern and unforgiving. He broke off the engagement with his fiancée who was living in the manor at the time. She was distraught and heartbroken and died shortly thereafter. The sounds of her sorrowful weeping are part of the residual haunting still heard today.

I did not find a mention of Captain Billopp's wife, but the official Web site for Conference House states that he had two daughters, Mary and Anne. Anne married Colonel Thomas Farmar in 1705. Their third son, Thomas, was born in 1711. He assumed the Billopp name and inherited the manor and the estate. Thomas and his second wife, Sarah Leonard, had eight children. Their eldest son was Christopher, named for his great-grandfather. Christopher became Colonel of Loyalist troops during the Revolutionary War.

My research shows conflicting stories regarding the death of a servant girl in the house. One story relates that Colonel Christopher Billopp was romantically involved with a female slave or servant. One night they argued, and in a fit of rage he drove a knife into her chest, she fell down the stairs and bled to death. The other story names Captain Christopher Billopp as having made sexual advances towards a female slave. When she rejected his advances, he stabbed her with a fireplace poker on the landing of the stairway. In either situation, the legend remains that at night this scene replays itself audibly with laughter which turns to screams of terror and concludes with an eerie silence.

September 11, 1776 is the namesake date of the Conference House as on that date Benjamin Franklin, John Adams, and Edward Rutledge convened at Colonel Billopp's house to negotiate for peace with Lord Admiral Richard Howe, who was sent from England to represent the king. Howe was instructed to deliver the message that independence would not be granted and after three hours of conferring, the message was received. The Americans quickly departed to prepare for the inevitable war.

During the Revolutionary War, Colonel Billopp remained loyal to Britain. He was kidnapped by the Americans several times before he suspected that he was being betrayed by someone in his own home. Supposedly, he caught a servant girl placing a lantern in an upstairs bedroom window which faced towards Perth Amboy, New Jersey. He was furious and chased the girl. It is not clear if he shoved her down the stairs or if she lost her footing and fell down the stairs, but she did break her neck as a result of falling down the stairs. Therefore, we can add her terri- fied spirit to the *guest list* at the Conference House.

Several British soldiers who were buried in the basement are reported to send unnerving chills down the backs of those who enter the basement to this day. Perhaps their spirits cannot rest since their remains are interred on "enemy soil."

Eventually, Colonel Billopp relocated to Nova Scotia, Can- ada, because his manor, along with other Loyalist properties, was seized by the state of New York. Afterwards, the house was privately owned, and, at one point, housed a rat poison com- pany before the house fell into disrepair. In1926, the Confer- ence House Association was created to restore the structure and make it suitable as a museum open to the public in an effort to preserve this part of American history.

In 1962, paranormal expert Hans Holzer investigated Con- ference House, accompanied by the renowned psychic medium Ethel Meyers. Ethel was not given any information about the place beforehand, yet she detected the murder of a female on the stairs and the trapped souls in the basement. She also sensed past use of the tunnel under the house, which had indeed been used to bring in supplies in from the shore because it offered protection from inclement weather and Indian attacks. Ten years later, Holzer asked the psychic Ingrid Beckman to visit Conference House by herself. She knew only the account of what Ethel Meyers had seen in 1962. While on the front porch of the house, Beckman experienced the sensation of being watched. Once inside, she was stopped in her tracks in the basement by a chill from where she felt the British were buried. Upstairs, she felt that the spirit of a woman was connected to the upstairs bedroom, the stairwell, and possibly the tunnel. Beckman went back to Conference House the following year, in 1973, and spoke with the caretaker, who had some interesting insights to share. On the anniversary of the murder of the young slave or servant girl, the caretaker saw a girl standing on the first landing of the stairs and a man running up the stairs toward her. Once the caretaker's daughter spent the night in the house and reported hearing the sound of a man laughing, then a woman laughing followed by a chilling scream. To comfort her daughter, the care-taker told her it was an "audio tape" that plays regularly, and that she should not be alarmed by it.

The best story I've seen about a ghostly encounter at the Con-ference House was told by a young girl named Margaret who, along with her grandmother, visited the historic site for a tour in 1951. While her grandmother was engaged in conversation with the tour guide, Margaret wandered upstairs by herself. In the parlor, she saw a man seated in a chair in the corner. Figuring the man was another staff member or tour guide, she asked him about the room and its history, but he quickly vanished. Marga-ret was baffled, as she did not see where he went, nor did she hear him walk across the squeaky floorboards. Within seconds, the man reappeared, and Margaret persisted with her questions. He answered them directly, but with a voice that seemed to ema-nate from all around her. The man then asked Margaret ques-tions about herself. According to Therese Lanigan-Schmidt's book *Ghosts of New York City*, he also asked, "What is General

Washington doing now about the British?" Margaret knew that George Washington had been the first President of the United States and that he had died years ago. She informed the man that Harry Truman was president and that the year was 1951. Margaret later said that the man quickly sat down upon hearing the information, appearing completely dumbfounded as he faded from view.

Having visited Conference House in the light of day, I can say the grounds are beautiful and the view of the Raritan Bay is breathtaking. Although I tried to collect EVPs, I found none. I decided to revisit Conference House at night to see if my luck would improve. The night my son and I went, the weather was partly cloudy. It was also quite humid, the ground being very wet from a Nor'easter the week before, and rain was forecast for the next day. The temperature outside was about fifty degrees, and the moon was a waxing crescent.

As Brian and I approached the front of the Conference House, I took pictures and recorded for EVPs with the digital audio recorder. Brian was recording video with his Sony DVD camcorder, using its NightShot® mode. Three teenage males walked past us down to the dock area. Every so often I could hear their laughter, but for the most part, the grounds were very quiet save for the sounds of twigs snapping under our feet as we walked.

We walked down the path along the side of the herb garden. We heard a loud rumbling noise, figuring it was a train off in the distance. Then an airplane flew over us, and I noted this on the recording. I find it's always a good idea to note on your audio recording the sounds you hear in the distance such as voices, traffic, and things you step on or bump into. That way, when you're reviewing your data, you won't waste time wondering what a sound was and whether it was a genuine EVP.

We went back to the house. Brian walked around the side of the house that faces toward the visitors' center, where we had parked. I stayed on the front porch and recorded for EVPs. After ten minutes, I walked down toward the water and asked aloud whether Captain Christopher Billopp would like to speak with me. I heard no response, either at the time or later when reviewing. However, at time index 17:25 on my recording, I say to Brian, "I think we can make our way back to the car." Then a breathy sound like "hi" is heard, after which my son replies to me, "Do you think we got anything? Any EVP?" I honestly thought we had an EVP greeting us with the word "Hi," but after watching Brian's video of the same moment, I realized the sound had actually been Brian clearing his throat.

I did see some orbs in the fifty-two photos I took that night, but I can't count those as paranormal given the wet grass and the dusty gravel path we had been walking on. Although Brian and I didn't document anything paranormal with video, photos, or audio, I have the feeling that Captain and Colonel Billopp were simply off duty that night, not fully retired. I plan to return to Conference House when it reopens for weekend tours in the late spring. Perhaps I'll be lucky enough then to have a chat with one of the Billopps like the one young Margaret had.

# CHAPTER 13

# Ellis and Liberty Islands

THERE'S NO MORE SIGNIFICANT SYMBOL of New York City than the Statue of Liberty. Designed by Frederic-Auguste Bartholdi and gifted to the United States by France, Lady Liberty was originally intended to welcome arriving immigrants, but that function was delegated to Ellis Island. She was also tasked with being a lighthouse because of her torch, which was lit by electric bulbs—a technology that was a year old at the time the torch was illuminated. However, as one of the park rangers at the monument put it, "She amounted to a night-light, as the brightest bulb at that time was 20 watts."

The statue arrived in New York harbor in 1885 and remained there for a year, awaiting a place to stand. One park ranger I spoke with explained that it had been America's responsibility to build a pedestal for the statue, but that people from other states viewed the statue as a "New York item" and therefore didn't care to donate money for the project. Finally, in 1886, the lady was in place on her pedestal and serving as a lighthouse, if a rather dim one.

Ellis Island is a historically rich place to visit. There has been some controversy over which state actually owns it: New Jersey or New York. Back in the 1600s, the island was smaller and was part of New Amsterdam, which is now New York City. Later, the size of the island was increased to twenty-seven acres using landfill brought from Brooklyn; however, the increase in the island's size stretched it into New Jersey waters, and the Supreme Court ruled in 1998 that Ellis Island is now "mostly New Jersey's territory." According to a park ranger, "If you're inside the museum, you're in New York. Once you step outside, you're in New Jersey."

Ellis Island was the arrival point in America for more than twelve million immigrants between 1892 and 1954. Upon arrival, immigrants were inspected for disease and mental illness. If a white "X" was chalked on a person's lapel, he was sent to the psychiatric ward for further evaluation; this happened to nine out of every hundred immigrants, according to a display at the Ellis Island Museum. One part of the examination that I can only imagine must have been brutally painful was the use of button hooks to turn the immigrants' eyelids inside out to inspect for trachoma, a highly contagious form of pinkeye. It is estimated that 250,000 immigrants were rejected for various reasons and sent back to where they had come from. According to a *New York Times* article, "In half a century, 355 babies were born here, and 3,500 immigrants died, including three suicides." The statistics add up to a high level of emotional turmoil and stress that no doubt left a psychic imprint on the island.

In 1954, Ellis Island ceased serving as the point of entry for immigration. Ten years later, the only signs of life on the island were a Doberman pinscher named "Topper," who lived there, and "pirates" who ransacked the thirty abandoned buildings and stole portable items such as desks and chairs. Thanks to the National Parks Service and a not-for-profit group called Save Ellis Island, restoration was undertaken, and the main building was opened as a museum on September 10, 1990. In 2007, the ferry building was completely restored and opened to the public. Currently, funding is being sought to restore the hospital and its various wards. As noted in a September 8, 2001 *New York Times* article, "Despite the deterioration, the hospital complex remains a handsome example of the golden age of public architecture, with copper gutters, skylights clad in terra cotta and interior doorways trimmed out in marble."

The tour of Ellis and Liberty Islands is by far the best value of all the wonderful things one can do in New York City. Just twelve dollars buys one adult ticket for the Statue Cruise ferry, which runs between Liberty State Park, New Jersey, and Battery Park, New York City, and stops at both islands. There is a slight additional fee to climb the steps inside the statue and enter the crown. You can make an entire day out of the visit. Coolers are not allowed, but brown-bag lunches are, making this a very affordable trip for an entire family.

My son Brian and I visited Ellis and Liberty Islands in February 2010. Being there during the off-peak season meant that we were frequently alone, so I had several opportunities to record for EVP. Of the eight recording attempts I made, not one yielded a positive result for EVP. This was disappointing; I thought surely we would capture something in the third-floor stairwell, which was very quiet and sequestered.

Brian and I perused the bookstore on the main level of the museum looking for books related to ghosts on Ellis Island. Finding none, I asked the sales clerk if she had any in stock. She said that the "ghost angle" was frowned upon at this historic site and that therefore the bookstore was prohibited from selling such books. She confided in me, however, that she loves "that stuff" and would definitely buy such a book if one were available. Seeing that she had a genuine interest in the topic, I asked her if she ever had any paranormal experiences while working there. She said that she hadn't personally, but that she had heard several times from the cleaning crew that they hear voices and people milling around late at night. They look for the source of these sounds but find no one there. This sales clerk also told me that a cleaning person witnessed a full-body apparition outside the window next to the bookstore. The ghost was described as a young man walking and carrying a stick on his shoulder with a sack tied to the end of it.

Brian and I sat outside Theater 1 and took several pictures of the entrance to the restrooms; I also recorded for EVP. We chose this spot because I'd heard about an incident that happened there. A woman at a New Jersey Ghost Hunter's Society meeting in 1999 reported that she and her sister had taken their children to visit Ellis and Liberty Islands. While at Ellis Island, the woman and her daughter went to the ladies' room on the first floor, outside Theater 1. She finished ahead of her daughter and went out into the hall to wait for her. A few minutes later, the child came running out, upset and frightened, saying there was a man in the restroom. The woman reported this to security, who inspected the restroom but found no one. Once the girl calmed down, she described the man from his head down almost to his toes. I say "almost" because that's what scared the child the most: the man's legs were invisible from the knees down.

Years after hearing that story, I heard from another mother who asked me if Ellis Island was haunted. She was curious because when she visited it with her family, her son had an encounter. She said that she was perusing the displays and

**The infirmary/hospital on Ellis Island**

noticed her son had wandered off. She found him seemingly engaged in conversation with a blank wall. When she asked him who he was talking to, he said, "This man." She looked, and her son turned to point out the gentleman, but he was gone. The mother asked her son what the man had said, and her son told her of the man's journey to America aboard a ship and his arrival at Ellis Island. The boy also said that it was hard to understand the man because he had an accent and didn't speak English well. The details her son relayed were well beyond his scope of knowledge. Furthermore, the boy was not scared at all. He was certain that he had spoken with a real man, although he was puzzled as to how the man disappeared so quickly.

Whether the historians want to admit it or not, Ellis Island is haunted. I will definitely go back when the hospital and psychiatric wards are restored and opened for tours.

After our tour of Ellis Island, Brian and I boarded the 2:30 P.M. ferry from there to Liberty Island, where the statue is. There is an interesting history to Liberty Island. It was originally called Bedlow's Island (sometimes spelled Bedloe's). In 1699, supposedly the infamous Captain Kidd buried some of his treasure on the island. In colonial days, the island was used to quarantine smallpox sufferers, and in 1800, star-shaped Fort Wood, from which the Statue of Liberty's pedestal rises, was built here.

One of the earliest ghost stories associated with Bedlow's Island is based on a treasure hunt that took place at Fort Wood in 1825. One Sargent Gibbs, along with a new recruit named Carpenter, set out at midnight during a full moon to dig for Captain Kidd's treasure, which they planned to locate using a divining rod made from witch hazel. Using a shovel and pick that they had previously hidden outside the fort, the two men began their excavation at the spot their divining rod indicated. They were excited when they struck a metal box just four feet below the surface, but their excitement vanished quickly when a brightly lit demonic entity rose up from the hole. Gibbs described it as black and horned with wings on its shoulders and a barbed tail. He said it breathed fumes of sulfur into his face and tossed him into the bay. Carpenter said the entity was red, without wings or legs and that it "moved without visible means of locomotion." The men screamed, attracting the attention of fort sentries who arrived moments later to discover Gibbs lying unconscious in the water and Carpenter fleeing in terror. Both Carpenter and Gibbs were turned over to the sergeant-at-arms for being outside the fort walls without permission. While the two men gave different descriptions of the entity they had seen, they did agree on its likely source: According to legend, Kidd had buried one or two of his crew along with with his treasure to guard it.

Two years after the incident with Carpenter and Gibbs, an enlisted man named Gardner was ordered to stand guard at Fort Wood from 11 P.M. to 2 A.M. This man had previously boasted that he would have been a great partner to Gibbs and Carpenter. However, his true timid nature was displayed when he was frightened by a ghost that seemed to rise up from between two graves. The same thing happened on his watch several nights in succession, but finally the "ghost" was apprehended: It was a Corporal Duvanny, who had a grudge against Gardner and chose to scare him by wearing a sheet and hiding in the cemetery.

Suicides have occurred on Liberty Island. The first happened forty-three years after the statue was installed. Ralph Gleason, twenty-two years old, jumped to his death from the crown of the statue; his body landed a few feet from where a worker was mowing the lawn. One witness said he saw Gleason climb out of a window, then turn as if to go back inside. Sadly, he slipped, fell and bounced off the chest of the statue before completing the 200-foot fall. A park ranger I spoke with at the entrance of the stairway to the crown mentioned this suicide. According to him, Gleason's suicide was related to the great stock market crash of October 1929. However, upon researching it, I found that this suicide had taken place in May of 1929. I also discovered that there had been an unsuccessful suicide attempt three years prior. A young Russian refugee wanted to jump to his death rather than face deportation, but a corporal on duty prevented the jump.

A second suicide occurred at Liberty Island on June 1, 1997. Thirty-year-old Elhajo Malick Dieye appeared distressed and upset when he was told by Sgt. C.J. Ross that the stairs to the crown were closed for the day, as it was after 5:30 P.M. Dieye insisted on reaching the crown to escape the F.B.I. agents who were chasing him. When Sgt. Ross moved towards Dieye to escort him safely down the stairs, Dieye turned and ran out the door, then jumped over the wall, falling five stories to his death.

Ellis Island as seen from the ferry

Two deaths more loosely linked to the Statue of Liberty than those suicides but no less tragic occurred on October 11, 2006. New York Yankees pitcher Cory Lidle and his flight instructor, Tyler Stanger, had taken off in a small plane from Teterboro Airport in New Jersey. The plane circled the Statue of Liberty before proceeding north up the East River and crashing into a high-rise apartment building.

When I visied the Statue of Liberty, a park ranger stationed at the entrance to the crown said, "In the 123 years the statue has been open to the public, we've averaged between four and six million visitors a year. So the Statue of Liberty has a very safe track record." Safe, yes, but is it haunted? I vote yes. Water, which of course surrounds the statue, conducts electricity, providing a perfect amplifier for the energy spirits need in order to manifest. The statue also rests atop a former fort whose history includes stories of ghostly pirates and their treasure.

Metaphysical properties factor into the statue's haunted energy as well. The fort underneath Lady Liberty's pedestal is in the shape of an eleven-pointed star. In numerology, eleven is a "double master number," meaning it does not reduce to a two, and eleven is the number of visionaries and leaders (in fact, George Washington was a double master eleven). There are seven points in Liberty's crown, and seven is the number of spirituality in numerology. According to adherents of a group of texts called the Ascended Master Teachings,there is keen spiritual representation in the crown, described as follows in the book *The Seven Mighty Elohim Speak On: The Seven Steps to Precipitation,* by Thomas Printz: "The first ray is represented at the left side of the forehead by the blue flame of Hercules; then follows the sunshine-yellow flame of Cassiopea; then the pink flame of Orion. The center flame on the front of the crown is the crystal flame of Cosmic Christ Purity, within which is held a focus of the All-Seeing-Eye of God. Around the flame there ascends a radiance of the Ray to which the individualized lifestream belongs. Next there follows the Green flame of Vista; the Golden flame of the Elohim of Peace, ending on the right side of the forehead with the Violet flame of Arcturus." The book also maintains that all humans have this "crown of Elohim" on their foreheads, but only those who have mastered their "inner sight" can see it. Perhaps Bartholdi channeled his inner sight and wisdom into the sculpting of this statue and its "crown of Elohim." As a ghost hunter, I feel it's important to examine all the possible energies and metaphysical properties of a haunting; you never know what might be acting as a conduit or amplifier to the great beyond. Knowing what you now know about the crown, go visit the Statue of Liberty. Investigate traditionally by recording for EVPs and taking pictures, but also pay attention to the subtle energies there.

# CHAPTER 14

# Richmond Town

THIS BEAUTIFUL HISTORIC VILLAGE on 100 acres of land, located at 441 Clark Avenue, is the result of relocating several buildings from around Staten Island. Time periods depicted via the buildings and furnishings range from the seventeenth century to the twentieth. Tour guides and artisans in period clothing complete the experience of stepping back in time. Of course, that may just complicate matters if you're wondering, "Was that a full-body apparition or a real person?"

My sons and I took the tour of Richmond Town on March 6, 2010. We first went to the Voorlezer's House, built in 1695 by the Dutch Reformed Congregation. The Voorlezer was the community's record keeper, schoolmaster, and lay minister. The title "Voorlezer," loosely translated from Dutch, means "one who

The study at the Guyen-Lake-Tysen House. Note the orb in the right corner of the picture.

stands before and reads." During the winter months, children went to school in the Voorlezer's house. While the docent for our tour explained and demonstrated the various tools used for discipline, I kept my audio recorder on in hopes of catching an EVP. Since this was a farming community, children worked on their families' farms during the spring, summer, and fall. On Sundays, church services were held upstairs.

Visitors are not allowed to venture upstairs because the structure is unsafe. Our docent took us into the Voorlezer's bedroom and showed us a corner of the flooring that is original, circa 1695. She also explained that the bedroom was the only personal space for the Voorlezer and his family. They slept, ate, and entertained guests in this one small room; the rest of the house belonged to the community.

From the Voorlezer's House we traveled past the foundation of an old farm house and arrived at the tavern, which was built in 1819. Just prior to our arrival, the potbellied stove had been stoked to warm the place for the evening performances. The ventilation pipe leading from the stove had a crack in it, and smoke was seeping out into the room. Of course, the smoky air meant picture-taking for paranormal anomalies was out of the question. Collecting EVPs was impossible because we had to leave the front door open to vent the smoke, and the street traffic was loud.

Thankfully, we left the smoky tavern quickly and went over to the Guyon-Lake-Tysen House. Joseph Guyon built the original portion of this house in 1740 on his 112-acre farm. He incorporated a Dutch door to allow light and air into the kitchen while keeping animals outside. A custom-fitted iron "arm" in the hearth was hinged so that it could swivel out from the fire, allowing easy and safe adding or removal of cooking pots. According to the docent, the fact that this arm was custom-made indicates the family was wealthy. This was an innovative and uncommon fixture to have in one's home at that time.

Over the years, tour guides at the Guyon-Lake-Tysen House have reported feeling as if they were not alone in the home even when they knew they were. Staff have also heard someone walking on the second floor at times they knew no one else was there. A few times, when the house was closed to the public, people reported seeing children in the house, leading to closer inspections that uncovered nothing. To those strange occurrences, add cupboard doors that open on their own, toys and bedspreads that are found not as they were left, doors that open freely one moment and refuse to budge the next, and paranormal odors that briefly arise and then vanish—and you have yourself an actively haunted house.

During our tour, I noticed that a broom stood inverted in the corner between the window and the door of the servant's staircase. I asked the docent if the broom was always positioned like that. She said she never really noticed it before. I told her I thought it was odd to leave it standing upside down like that, as it's an old custom to invert a broom to rid one's home of unwanted visitors or guests who have overstayed their welcome. I myself used this "trick" when I owned a bookstore. If someone came in who made me uncomfortable, I would excuse myself and go to the office part of the store, invert my little broom, then return to the front counter, and within minutes the person would leave. I would then return my broom to its bristles-down position. Our docent, flipping the broom in the corner to the welcoming position, said, "I did not know that. I'll have to try it out."

We continued past the pantry and into Guyon's parlor and bedroom area. We noted nothing paranormal here. Next, we went into the main foyer where the grandfather clock is located. We were allowed to go upstairs and see the bedrooms, each of which is furnished in a different time period. We were not allowed to walk into the rooms that were the slaves' quarters; the docent warned us that the floors there were so weak, we would end up crashing through to the kitchen below. Just before the doorway to the slaves' quarters is a child's bedroom. I felt uneasy in this area, yet I couldn't understand why, as the room was sunny and cheerful-looking. Later, when I reviewed my photos on the computer, I noticed the faint, ghostly face of a man in the mirror atop the dresser in that bedroom.

The final stop on the tour was the General Store, which was built by Stephen D. Stephens in 1840. Joseph Black took over as owner in 1870, and he and his three daughters operated the store and post office until 1918. The building suffered fire damage in 1944 and was reconstructed in 1964 from historic photographs and research. Many of the artifacts are not original to the store, but they complete the presentation perfectly. Over the years, there have been reports of unidentifiable knocking sounds here.

Child's bedroom at the Guyen-Lake-Tysen House. Note the ghostly face in the mirror on the dresser.

The Parsonage House, originally the home of the Dutch Reformed Church minister, was built in 1855. It became a private residence in 1875, and in more recent years it has been known as the Parsonage House Restaurant. Currently, the restaurant is closed and in between owners, but I managed to speak with Brian Cano, of the *Scared!* online television series, about his team's 2005 investigation there. Brian's team had permission to investigate the restaurant after business hours. They spoke with a couple of busboys who said they had experienced menacing male spirit energy in the attic and preferred not to go up there. The busboys also reported being tapped on the shoulder, as if by a customer or co-worker needing their attention, only to turn and find no one there. They had even seen items such as flatware levitate and fly off tables.

Upon hearing all this, Brian's team was set for an exciting evening of paranormal investigating. When they went into the attic, they felt anxious and in a hurry to get out. They heard scratching noises there that they couldn't attribute to conventional causes such as squirrels, rats, mice, or tree branches hitting the roof.

The *Scared!* team also conducted EVP sessions in the restaurant. Brian said, "Can you give us a sign of your presence?" As if on cue, the restaurant's phone rang. Brian answered the phone, and no one was there.

After a long night, the team decided to call it quits and began to pack up their equipment. Suddenly, Brian's new EMF detector registered a signature in the center of the living room about four and a half feet off the ground. He described it as a "bubble" of EMF readings. "You could go to the left and it would stop, or go to the right and lose the EMF signature," he told me. "I tried to get a reading close to the floor, figuring wiring at the ceiling of the basement would register, but no signature was detected. Back up to about 4.5 feet off the floor, and there it was again." Brian's team and their psychic followed this EMF bubble as it moved up the stairs and to the attic door, where it dissipated. They went into the attic to see if the energy was there, but it wasn't.

At the conclusion of my tour of Richmond Town, I asked the docent if she had heard any ghost stories or had any paranormal experiences while working there. She said, "I've heard a lot of stories of ghosts associated with the various buildings over the years. I've been working here for fourteen years. I'm a skeptic; I can't accept the ghost stories until I experience it for myself. I wish just once something would happen to me while I'm working here." And so I close this chapter with some sound advice: Be careful what you wish for!

# CHAPTER 15

# Snug Harbor

ACCORDING TO ITS WEBSITE, www.snug-harbor.org, Snug Harbor Cultural Center and Botanical Garden is "Staten Island's premier destination for culture and entertainment." Affiliated with the Smithsonian Institution and located in "a stunning 83-acre park-like setting," Snug Harbor "presents a unique blend of gardens, museums, theaters, educational opportunities, and seasonal festivals." Walking through the gardens, relaxing in the gazebo, or meditating while meandering through the pond area, one would never suspect the frightening energies hidden within Snug Harbor's Monet-come-to-life tranquility.

In 1801, wealthy Robert Randall, son of a merchant seaman, provided in his will for a safe haven where "aged, decrepit and worn-out" seamen could retire. His 140-acre farm became that haven in 1833 when a hospital and home were built on the property for retired seamen of any nation. The only rules of occupancy were that retired sailors had to attend prayer services, say grace before every meal, maintain sobriety, and be in bed by 9 P.M. The place was named Sailor's Snug Harbor.

From 1867 to 1884, Captain Thomas Melville, brother of *Moby Dick* author Herman Melville, was governor at Sailor's Snug Harbor. By 1900, approximately 1,000 retired sailors lived there. It was an ideal place for them: the facility was self-contained, with churches, farmland, and a theater, yet it was close to the water, a comforting sight for the "old salts." As time passed, the population at Sailor's Snug diminished. Eventually, the City of New York took possession of the property. In 1976, the remaining 110 sailors were relocated to Sea Level, North Carolina.

I visited Snug Harbor in May 2009. It was a clear evening, warm but not muggy. Brian Backstrom, a security guard who has worked at Snug Harbor for the past eleven years, guided me through the various buildings. This young man had not only his own paranormal experiences at Snug Harbor to tell me about, but a wealth of historical information as well.

We started at the Music Hall. Brian told me that this theater was the second oldest in New York City, "the first being Carnegie Hall." We entered the theater and, per my request, Brian kept the lights off. I used my camcorder in "night shot" mode to look for any possibly paranormal anomalies. Additionally, I used a thermal scanner to check for temperature drops, and I took pictures with my Nikon digital camera.

I followed Brian down the main aisle to arrive in front of the stage. Rumor has it that a man had committed suicide backstage by climbing to the catwalks and hanging himself with a stage rope. It was one of those tales of unrequited love: supposedly he was a retired sailor who fell in love with Mrs. Randall and, realizing he could not have her, ended his life. Brian said he had tried to research the story in the institution's archives before they were transferred to North Carolina for storage, but he was unable to confirm it. The rumor is perpetuated, however, by various performing artists who claim to have seen the shadow of a nonexistent dangling figure on the left stage wall.

Brian told me about an experience he had in the music hall back when he was employed with the maintenance staff. "It was around 11 P.M., and I was vacuuming this area of the theater [stage left, rows 4 to 6] when I heard a crash behind me. I turned around and saw the light rigging had been pushed from the balcony it was attached to and slammed right into the floor. It missed hitting me by two rows!" Needless to say, Brian did not finish vacuuming that night.

I wandered backstage and took some recordings and photos, but I didn't capture anything paranormally suspicious.

From the Music Hall, we went over to Building K, called the Matron's House. The story attached to this building is disturbing. According to the story, at one time the Head Matron had "adopted"—enslaved, really—a local teenage boy who was mildly retarded. She kept him chained like an animal in the basement of the Matron's House. One day, the boy managed to free himself and made his way to the main floor. He grabbed a pair of sewing shears and proceeded to the Head Matron's bedroom on the third floor. He stabbed her multiple times and fled toward Forrest Avenue, but he was captured and brought back to Snug Harbor, where he was hanged from the "hanging tree" which is in back of Building K.

The "hanging tree" is notable not only for its namesake function, but also for the rather ghastly-looking spiked branches that grow around its trunk. Brian said numerous trees on the property have been struck by lightning or felled by wind over the years, yet the "hanging tree" remains unscathed.

**The Governor's House at Snug Harbor**

Although I did not capture any anomalies in pictures or video in the Matron's house, I did experience an unusual battery drain on the camcorder in the Head Matron's former bedroom on the third floor. Luckily, I had a fully charged spare, which I installed once we were outside the building.

After taking pictures of the Hanging Tree, we walked to Building L, where Brian had a strange experience in the fall of 2005. He and another park ranger were standing there engaged in conversation, he said, just as he and I were at that moment. It was approximately 11 P.M. and no one else was with them. Suddenly, a bizarre creature darted between them, headed toward Building L, and disappeared into the ground. Brian described the animal as about the size of a Labrador dog with the hindquarters of a rabbit and the head of a wild dog or "hell hound." Brian said it made a high-pitched shriek as it vanished into the ground approximately twenty feet from where he and the other ranger stood.

Brian and the other man did not discuss with each other what they had witnessed. Independently, however, they both confided in their sergeant about the experience, and the details of their accounts were identical.

We continued to the storm door at the entrance to Building K's basement. Spiders and cockroaches the size of small puppies added to the subterranean ambiance as we made our way downstairs. Brian showed me the area where the teenage boy had supposedly been shackled to the wall. Odd-shaped metal loops protruded from the wall, but it was unclear whether they were the remnants of shackles. I took several pictures with no apparent paranormal results save for a dust orb. The temperature remained constant at 58 degrees, according to my thermal scanner.

We then climbed the stairs out of the Building K basement and made our way to the Governor's House. This is the beautiful, Victorian-style building one sees upon driving into Snug Harbor. Brian pointed out a window on the second floor that had a vantage point of the harbor back when the house was constructed. However, trees on the property now obscure the view. Brian said many visitors and park rangers have reported seeing a ghostly white figure in this window. Possibly the classic Lady in White resides eternally in the Governor's House. Some suspect she is the former Mrs. Robert Randall, but this theory is doubtful given that the house was built long after the Randalls lived there. However, the Randalls' son, Richard, was a bachelor, and he could have had a mistress or two in residence at the house.

According to Brian, the ghostly woman in white has been seen coming out through the front door and making her way around the side of the house to the path that leads down the road. It is suspected that she is attempting to visit a cemetery that used to be there. In recent years, the cemetery was relocated to a spot approximately two blocks away.

Brian led me into the Governor's House via the front door. It appeared that the beautiful structure was now being used as

**Security guard Brian Backstrom has worked at Snug Harbor for eleven years—plenty of time for some paranormal experiences.**

a storage unit. Tables, folding chairs, and other equipment was strewn about the two front rooms or parlors. I went to the second floor to record for EVPs and noted an alarm going off in the background. Brian said it was a motion sensor alarm and that it frequently goes off even when no one is in the house.

I went to the window where the lady in white had been spotted. Thermal scanning showed a constant temperature of 71.4 degrees Fahrenheit. I did not collect any EVPs, and there were no anomalies in my digital still shots of the house.

A dance class, in the same building as Brian's office, had ended just as I was wrapping up my day at Snug Harbor. The landscape that had looked so sunny and inviting when I arrived had a much more foreboding, somewhat menacing appearance now that it was evening. I got into my car and joined the procession of cars that were also leaving. Honestly, I was thankful for their company.

# CHAPTER 16

# Van Cortlandt House

THIS HISTORIC HOME WAS BUILT on property originally purchased from the Mohegan Indians by Adriaen Van der
Donck in 1646. In 1748, Van Cortlandt house became part of
the sprawling estate, wheat farm, and grist mill of Frederick Van
Cortlandt, son of Jacobus. This is another of the many places
where General George Washington slept. He used the house as
his headquarters in 1776 and at the beginning and end of his
presidential campaign in 1783.

The house left the Van Cortlandt family in 1896 when the
entire property was sold to the City of New York. The National
Society of Colonial Dames in the State of New York worked to
restore the house and make it a museum. Members of the Van
Cortlandt family donated furnishings so that the museum would

reflect eighteenth-century life as accurately as possible. Today, the 262-year old home is listed as a National Historic Landmark and a New York City Landmark.

Above each front window of the house is a hideous carved stone face, or gargoyle. Placed specifically to ward off evil spirits from a home, gargoyles were quite common in the Netherlands, where the Van Cortlandts were from, but they were certainly a rarity here in the United States. Some claim that the stone grimaces at Van Cortlandt House have worked as intended, and that only good spirits reside here.

Two instances of ghostly encounters stand out in the history of Van Cortlandt House. The first occurred before it was a museum. A young girl who was visiting her aunt and uncle, the then-owners of the mansion, was sleeping in the children's playroom, which was separate from the main part of the house. She was woken during the night by the sound of footsteps fast approaching her door. Suddenly the door opened, and the girl sat up in bed to see the figure of a woman, short in stature, standing in the doorway. The woman was dressed in a brown skirt and cape with a cap on her head, and attached to her side was a set of keys that jangled. With a very quick pace, almost gliding, the woman came to the side of the girl's bed and tugged vigorously at the blankets. Terrified, the young girl pulled the covers up over her head and stayed that way until the morning, when the maid came in to wake her.

The next morning, the young girl described the frightening woman to her aunt and cousin. She had been unable to see the face; she was able to describe only what the woman had been wearing. The girl said she had heard a train whistle off in the distance at the time she thought the specter retreated, though she had been too scared to take her head out from under the covers to make sure. Her cousin said it had been the whistle of the 2 A.M. train, and that other guests had reported encountering the ghostly woman at the same hour.

The aunt and a friend of hers who claimed to be psychic conducted a séance, along with the young cousins, to determine the identity of this spirit. Supposedly they contacted the ghost of a former servant who was bound to the house because of her guilt at having stolen some silverware and a silver pie dish the Van Cortlandts had brought over from Holland. After the séance, the apparition was never seen again.

Other, less fortunate ghosts at Van Cortlandt House appear doomed to linger there, reliving their final days. For example, there is the ghost of a Hessian soldier who, in life, was tied to his bed to prevent him from hurting himself while he was severely intoxicated. Unfortunately, he spoke only German and therefore was unable to understand that what was being done to him was for his own good. His ghost returns periodically to the scene of his "torture." Another ghost, named Hannah, is more than likely a residual haunting. She is seen scouring the manor for the silver she hid during the Revolutionary War to prevent the British from confiscating it; unfortunately, she hid it so well that she couldn't find it at the conclusion of the war. The ghost of a British redcoat arrived at the house at the same time a wooden linen press was brought in; apparently his spirit was attached to the linen press and came with it. Two other female spirits have been experienced at the museum. Visitors report feeling a long dress drag past their legs as they walk up the main staircase, yet no one is visible. Also, people have seen a young girl arrive by horse-drawn carriage at the front of the manor, run up the front porch steps, and vanish. This, too, may be a residual haunting, as it sounds more like a recording replaying itself as opposed to a spirit displaying consciousness or interacting with the surroundings.

The final ghost to mention is that of Anne Stevenson Van Cortlandt, the last of the family to live in the manor. Apparently she was not happy about her family home being sold to

A protective stone face stares out above each
front window at the Van Cortlandt House.

outsiders, and she made her dissatisfaction known to one of the
workers renovating the manor in the 1940s. He clearly heard a
woman giving him orders but did not see anyone there. (Now,
that's not only paranormal; that's miraculous. A man heard a
woman!)

I visited Van Cortlandt House on March 10, 2010, with Dina
Chirico, team leader of the north Jersey division of the New Jersey Ghost Hunters' Society. The tour is self-guided, and we were
the only ones there, so it worked out perfectly. We were able to
take our time photographing, recording, and taking various
readings.

I didn't *feel* anything paranormal while in the house. A picture I took on the third floor while looking into the attic had a
white, cloudy appearance in one corner. I figured out that light
from the camera's flash had bounced off the white paint on the
doorframe into my lens. Dina and I sat on the stairs on the third
floor to review the tour guide manual and to record for EVP. We
found nothing notable in our recordings.

Online, however, I found a description of the recent experience of a girl named Jessica who visited Van Cortlandt House
with her father in May 2009. They entered the house as three
families were leaving, making them the only two people—well,

*living* people—in the house. While touring the first floor, they heard footsteps on the second floor. They assumed someone must have been touring the upstairs, but when they went upstairs, no one was there, and they hadn't passed anyone on the stairs. Jessica noted an exceptionally cold spot on the landing of the stairs. While upstairs, they heard the downstairs door open, followed by footsteps. Again, they wrote off what they had heard as attributable to more people entering the house to take the tour. Then they heard the door open and close again, and more footsteps. This time, though, the footsteps did not continue through the first floor, nor did they proceed up the stairs; they simply faded away. At this point, Jessica and her father exchanged perplexed expressions; Jessica said, "Did you hear that?" and her father replied, "Yeah." Her father called out a "hello," but no one answered.

In the children's room, Jessica noticed a doll on the table. Her father called her attention to something else, and when she looked back only seconds later to see the doll, it was on the opposite side of the room. As Jessica tried to process what she was seeing, she was overcome by an intense cold all around her. She knew at that point she'd been there long enough and urged her father to leave.

It's possible that Jessica felt the ghost of the woman on the stairs as an intense cold spot rather than as a gown grazing past her ankles. It's also possible that the ghost of Anne Van Cortlandt was straightening up the children's room and moved the doll, then hovered around Jessica as if to say, "What are you doing here?"

I spoke with the museum's director, Laura Carpenter, who has worked at the Van Cortlandt House since 1994. She told me her one and only strange experience there happened in 1997. She and a volunteer were working late in the house one night, around 10 P.M. They were moving furniture around to make room for holiday decorations. Suddenly, they both heard the sound of someone in heavy boots walking upstairs. Laura called out, "We're just working to make the house presentable," and the sound ceased. Still, she and the volunteer helper decided to call it a night, and they packed up their belongings and left.

Laura feels that her intuitive remark to the presence somehow worked to prevent it from ever coming around her again. "It's as if the spirit understood that I was there to take care of the home and was content with that knowledge. I haven't experienced anything since then," Laura explained.

While Dina and I did not experience or capture anything paranormal while at the Van Cortlandt House, the abundance of history and reported paranormal activity here keeps this house on the "must-visit" list for New York City ghost hunters.

# Museums

# CHAPTER 17

# Alice Austen House

ORIGINALLY BUILT AS A ONE-ROOM FARMHOUSE in 1690, "Clear Comfort," as it became known, expanded to a lovely Victorian cottage in 1844 when John Haggarty Austin purchased the property. Young Alice Austen came to live with her grandparents after her father abandoned her and her mother. Alice's uncle Oswald Miller taught her all about photography. At the age of ten, she was taking photographs and developing them in the darkroom with her uncle's supervision.

Alice's photojournalistic style was well ahead of its time. In fact, Alice was a rebel for her highly conservative Victorian time period. She was the first woman on Staten Island to own a car, and she could repair it herself. She was a master tennis player and landscape designer. She founded and was the first president of the Staten Island Garden Club. As noted in the Alice Austen Museum brochure, "Today, she might be the only woman in America, with the exception of Eleanor Roosevelt, to have a museum, ferry, school, and street named after her."

Sadly, Alice was forced to leave Clear Comfort in 1945 because of her financial situation and arthritis, which inhibited her passion for photography. Having never married, Alice died in 1952. Her home sat abandoned until a citizen's group banded together in the 1960s to save it. It is now a New York City Designated Landmark and a National Historic Landmark, and it is open to the public as a museum. Its location at 2 Hylan Boulevard still has the impressive and serene view of the New York Harbor and the Verrazano Narrows Bridge.

I visited the museum in March 2010. No docents were on duty when I arrived, so I could not interview anyone on staff. A group of teenagers was having a meeting in one of the rooms off the main gallery. True to teenage form, they were quite loud. Thankfully, when I was in the front parlor where the pump organ is, I was far enough away from the noise to do some EVP work.

The ghosts reported at the Alice Austen Museum are said to be those of Alice, her great-grandmother, and a British redcoat. Alice's great-grandmother cared for wounded British soldiers during the Revolutionary War, but one of her patients did not survive. According to Paranormal Investigations of Staten Island, who conducted a six-hour private investigation of the Alice Austen House, the paranormal activity reported here includes cold spots, disembodied voices, the paranormal odor of John Austin's cigar, an apparition in the caretaker's quarters, and movement of small objects including a portrait that hangs on an interior wall.

I did not capture any anomalies in my photos. I did, however, hear a female voice whispering something unintelligible on my audio recorder. I reviewed the voice path visually in my audio software to make sure the voice wasn't mine, and it definitely wasn't. However, I could not discern even one clear word in the disembodied whisper. It was probably a "Class C" EVP. Class A EVPs can be heard loud and clear without enhancements and without wearing headphones. Class B EVPs can be heard without headphones, but the voice may not be as loud and clear as a Class A. The faintest EVPs, those in Class C, are audible only with headphones, and it may be difficult to interpret all the words. A recording of someone mumbling in the next room would be equivalent to a Class C EVP.

After its six-hour investigation of the Alice Austen House, Paranormal Investigations of Staten Island concluded the following:

> In our analysis of the collected evidence we found no anomalous EVP recordings. None of the photographs taken produced evidence of activity. Video produced no evidence during our six hour investigation, as well as there were no anomalous readings in temperature. EMF base readings remained normal throughout the investigation. There were a couple personal experiences with anomalous cold spots; however, these were not able to be verified with our equipment. The scent of cigars was not experienced by any investigator and therefore could not be verified.
>
> It is in our opinion, that the evidence collected was insufficient to validate a claim of [the museum] being haunted. The only explanation, for the cigar smell, is that the area around the house is a public park so cigar smoke could enter the house even though there is no smoking permitted in or on the property.

I think that is stretching the cigar smoke conclusion a little too far. Cigar smoke is pungent and lingers, sometimes for days. Paranormal odors are there one minute and gone the next. If someone were smoking a cigar on the property, there would be enough odor to trace it to the source. Besides, visitors have reported smelling the cigar smoke inside the home, not wafting through a window from outside.

Granted, six hours is a lengthy investigation, but it certainly isn't long enough to write off a location as not haunted. The Alice Austen House may not be the most consistently active of paranormal hot spots, but I did capture a Class C EVP there, and I think the place has enough residual energies and sporadic manifestations to merit an inspection of your own.

I was able to speak with Paul Moakley, the caretaker and curator for the museum, who has lived and worked there for four years. When I asked him if he thought the place was haunted, he said, "I just feel a good presence there and have not had anything negative happen." Paul was kind enough to send me an 1878 article about the house that appeared in *Harper's*. It details the British redcoat's ghost as follows:

> A King George's man fell in love with a maiden who lived in [the house], and being rejected, desperately hanged himself from a beam in the ceiling, while she, like Charlotte in Thackeray's ballad, "went on cutting bread and butter." The disembodied spirit of this soft-hearted and soft-headed warrior still visits the chamber of his folly, and shamefully disturbs its occupants by the midnight clinking of his spurs and the tread of his double-soled boots.

I vote that you make an afternoon out of visiting the Alice Austen House museum. Pack a lunch along with your ghosthunting gear. When you're done touring the house and collecting evidence, enjoy your picnic lunch and the gorgeous view. Please do not leave any trash behind; don't expect the ghost of Alice or her great-grandmother to clean up after you.

# CHAPTER 18

# Garibaldi-Meucci Museum

LOCATED ON STATEN ISLAND, the Garibaldi-Meucci Museum houses historical displays and artwork and hosts Italian cultural classes. The museum also provides ghosthunters with paranormal activity to explore, but to fully understand it, we must get to know the two famous Italians for whom the museum is named.

Guiseppi Garibaldi is known as the George Washington of Italy. He fought for the unification of the twenty Italian city-states. Sadly for him, his hometown of Niza ended up becoming Nice, France, when the final borders of Italy were determined. In addition to fighting in Italy and being exiled, Garibaldi fought in South America in support of Brazil's war against Spain. It was in Brazil that he met the love of his life, Anita. They married and had four children together. Later, Garibaldi fought for Uruguay when it was invaded by Argentina. In Uruguay he was given a red shirt to wear, and this became the uniform for his fellow soldiers. They were known as "the Red Shirts."

Eventually Garibaldi returned to Italy with his wife and children so that he could fight once more to unite Italy. The Catholic states' army overwhelmed Garibaldi's men, and he was condemned to death. His wife had died during the battle; therefore, he left his children with his mother and fled to America to escape execution.

Antonio Meucci was born in Florence, Italy, and attended Accademia di Bell' Arte (the Academy of Fine Arts), where he studied chemical and mechanical engineering. He met his future wife, Ester Mochi, when she was a costume seamstress at a local opera company where he was working as a stage technician. They married in 1834, and in 1835, they moved with the opera company to Havana, Cuba. They stayed in Cuba for fifteen years before relocating to America in 1850. The home they rented, built ten years prior in 1840, eventually became the Garibaldi-Meucci Museum.

Meucci was a prolific inventor. In fact, he had a prototype for an electromechanical telephone when Alexander Graham Bell was only two years old. Although Meucci couldn't explain electricity—he was an inventor, not a scientist—he did discover that sound, encoded as electrical impulses, would travel over copper wires. In 1854, Meucci used his "teletrefono," as he called it, in his Staten Island home. The device allowed his wife, who was ill and bedridden, to call from her bedroom to his workshop if she needed something.

In 1860, Meucci didn't have the $250 necessary to secure a patent for his device. However, his lab partner at the time, Alexander Graham Bell, did have the money. Bell also had a powerful businessman named Hubbard as his future father-in-law. The well-connected Hubbard called in a favor or two that allowed his

Inventor Antonio Meucci is buried beneath this monument located on the front lawn of the museum, but his spirit seems to move about the property.

future son-in-law to submit for a patent for a tweaked version of Meucci's invention. Bell's design didn't work, yet he was allowed to correct and resubmit his application, and within three weeks the patent was granted. Even today, such a quick turnaround for a patent is unheard of. Curiously, Meucci's paperwork and designs disappeared from the patent office around the time Bell was submitting for the patent.

Meucci spoke only broken English, which cost him dearly in the effort to protect his business interests. He was truly taken advantage of by Bell and other big names of the day. For years, Meucci contested ownership of the telephone patent. Sadly, he died in 1899, before his case against Bell could be heard by the Supreme Court. But in 2002, the U.S. House of Representatives finally acknowledged Meucci as the inventor of the telephone.

So how were Garibaldi and Meucci connected? Garibaldi
arrived in New York shortly after the Meuccis had moved into
their home on Staten Island in 1850. Meucci insisted that Garibaldi stay with him and his wife, and Garibaldi ended up living
with the Meuccis for six months—although the plaque above
the entrance says he lived there for four years, probably because
he returned to Italy in 1854 to continue the fight for unification.

The house was moved to its present location in 1907, and a
pantheon structure was built over it to convert it to a temple paying homage to Garibaldi. The pantheon was removed in the early
1950s because it was deteriorating. When you enter the house
today, you're actually coming in the back door; the house was
rotated when placed on the property so that the sign announcing
Garibaldi as "Hero of Two Worlds" would face the street.

Meucci and his wife both died in residence at this house and
are buried on the property. It's possible that the rightfully dis-
gruntled energies of Meucci may account for the otherwise inexplicable banging noises sometimes heard there.

I spoke with Bonnie McCourt, publicity coordinator at the
museum, and she said that she has yet to experience anything
paranormal there. Her boss, Nichole, the museum director, is
relatively new to her post and has not encountered anything
unusual there either. Nichole did say, however, that her prede-
cessor had experienced cold spots and banging noises and was
once pushed by an unseen hand as she ascended the stairs on
her way to her second-floor office.

Nichole suggested I speak with Amy Raiola, Founder and
Lead Investigator for the Staten Island Paranormal Society. I did
just that. Amy first investigated the Garibaldi-Meucci Museum
in 2006. She told me that initially her team tracked a cold spot
that moved throughout the museum. In fact, just after they
entered the museum, it felt so cold that they decided to check the
furnace. One woman on the team opted to run back to her car to
retrieve her coat while the remaining team members inspected

**Antonio Meucci's death mask**

the furnace. By the time she got back into the museum with her coat, the place was hot—not just warmed up, but hot. Amy confirmed the furnace and heat were working properly. They realized that the cold spot moved around the museum, causing the furnace to run hotter than normal to compensate for the varying spots of extreme cold. Once the cold spot moved on, the space would revert back to being "extra toasty." The team also obtained photos of orbs and various EVP recordings.

In 2007, Amy and her team played host to Chris Moon of *Haunted Times* magazine and his Ghost Hunter's University. The investigation at the Garibaldi-Meucci Museum incorporated the "Spirit Com" communication device Moon developed based on Thomas Edison's original designs and ideas. Amy said it sounded as if voices from "the great beyond" were communicating via the "Spirit Com," but that no words were discernable. "It was very faint or garbled sounding," Amy said.

As the night wore on, several members of the team left the site to get something to eat. Amy and the remaining seven investigators continued their work. After a while, they called it quits and began packing up their equipment. Just as they had gotten everything packed and ready to be hauled to their cars, they heard a loud bang from upstairs in the library. Amy described it as the sound of a large television falling off its stand. The investigators rushed to the foot of the stairs. Amy was about to go upstairs to inspect, but she refrained, thinking it was probably one of the other investigators who was hiding up there and would jump out to scare her.

Another team member volunteered to go upstairs. When his foot landed on the third stair, they heard a woman's voice emanating from the top of the staircase, just outside the door to Garibaldi's room. The woman's voice was loud enough to be heard by everyone, but she was mumbling, so her words were not clear. Amy and a couple other investigators ran to their equipment cases and grabbed what they could. Chris Moon, with his audio recorder, was the first one upstairs. Amy followed with her camcorder.

Amy said her videocamera was working perfectly as she went up the stairs. As she approached the library, one of the investigators called out, "Matilda, is that you?" (Amy informed me that, over the course of their research, they had discovered the name "Matilda" in the museum's paperwork.) Chris Moon's audiorecorder captured the ghostly woman's response: "Yes." Right after that EVP, Amy's camcorder displayed lines across its screen and then shut down; it has not functioned since.

The day I went to the museum was not the best time to attempt to record for EVPs, though I tried. The offices on the

**Bonnie McCourt, publicity coordinator at the museum**


second floor were full of activity such as phone calls and a radio playing in the background. I heard a loud crash, but it was not a paranormal one; it was merely a stack of files on the edge of a counter falling to the floor.

Amy invited me to investigate the museum with her team the next time they go there. I simply cannot refuse. I want to know if Meucci's restless spirit is wandering there. Is he unaware of his posthumous recognition as the inventor of the telephone? Could the ghost of his wife be the mumbling woman at the top of stairs? Either way, Meucci should be proud . . . talk about a long-distance call!

# CHAPTER 19

# Merchant's House Museum

THE MERCHANT'S HOUSE was built in 1832; Seabury Tredwell purchased it in 1835. Tredwell had gained his wealth from the hardware import business he maintained on Pearl Street. At a time when New York City's downtown was fairly crowded, moving up to East Fourth Street indicated affluence.

The five-story brownstone was, and remains, a signature land-mark of Greek Revival architecture.

Tredwell was a stern parent to the eight children that his wife, Eliza, bore him. The two oldest daughters married, the two sons never amounted to anything, and the remaining four daughters—Mary, Phoebe, Sarah, and Gertrude—lived out their days in their father's house.

Born in 1840, Gertrude, nicknamed "Gittie", was the young-est of the Tredwell children and the only one to be born in the home. She fell in love with a medical student, Lewis Walton—"Lo," as she called him. Tredwell did not accept Lo: not only was he poor, he was Catholic as well. Tredwell, an Anglican, pres-sured Gertrude to break off the relationship with Lo. Out of spite, she declined all subsequent suitors her father suggested for her and never dated again.

There are two stories about Sarah that are disturbing but hard to prove. In both stories, she became pregnant out of wed-lock and feared her father's wrath. According to one version of the story, upon the birth of the baby, her father ordered a ser-vant to suffocate the newborn in the tunnel beneath the house. Sarah, rightfully depressed, walked along the East River inces-santly until she caught pneumonia and died. In the other ver-sion of the story, Sarah committed suicide rather than tell her father about the pregnancy.

Seabury Tredwell died in 1865, and the four spinster sisters remained in the home. One by one, they perished, with Phoebe's death the most tragic: she fell down the stairs and broke her neck. The last living sister, Gertrude, remained in the house alone, continuing her odd habits of shopping for food at night and keeping the shutters closed and the house dark at all times.

Although Gertrude kept the furnishings and decorations inside the house as she had known them while growing up, the world outside was changing—and not for the better. Industry

The staircase where
Phoebe Tredwell
tragically fell to her
death

had moved into the neighborhood, and the wealthy neighbors moved further uptown. Gertrude kept to herself and died in the upstairs bedroom in 1933 at the age of ninety-three.

On September 10, 2009, I had the pleasure of interviewing Anthony Bellov, a member of the Board of Directors for the Merchant's House Museum. He also wrote the booklet "Some Say They Never Left: Tales of the Strange and Inexplicable at the Merchant's House Museum." Bellov told me of an experience that took place in the servants' quarters in March 2009. Usually the servants' quarters are not open to the public, but the museum opened them for this particular St. Patrick's Day event because the servant population of the nineteenth century was largely Irish. A docent was upstairs on the fourth floor conducting a tour of the four bedrooms off the hallway. As the docent was beginning to usher the group down the stairs, she turned to glance back down the hallway and saw a woman peek her head out of one of the bedroom doors. The docent and the woman exchanged shocked glances before the woman abruptly withdrew into the bedroom and slammed the door shut. The docent hurried the tour group downstairs at a pace that was almost rude, as she could not get off that floor fast enough. It was several months before she could reveal her frightening experience to Anthony Bellov. She was positive that the woman she saw was a ghost.

The earliest sightings of a ghostly female visage date back to the period between Gertrude's death in 1933 and the opening of the museum in 1936. Most of the experiences happened to the workers who were employed to renovate the house into a functional museum. Several of them reported the feeling of being watched, and a few were so frightened they refused to return to work there, even though this was at the height of the Great Depression when jobs were scarce.

Around the same time, several children from the neighborhood tenement buildings were playing a loud game of stickball in the street in front of the house. Suddenly, the front door of the house opened and a petite elderly lady came running onto the front porch, admonishing the children and angrily shooing them away. A number of people in the neighborhood saw the little old lady and recognized her as the deceased Gertrude—so they were as shocked and frightened as the children.

Though there have not been any recent sightings of a ghostly woman on the staircase, over the years people have reported seeing a woman dressed in either brown or white clothing. There have also been reports of a woman in the kitchen staring out the back window toward the garden while drinking a cup of tea. Ghosthunters would consider the latter sighting a residual haunting because the apparition was not interactive or sentient, but was more like a recording playing as if on a loop tape.

Anthony told me about a couple from out of town who visited the museum. When they knocked on the door, a woman dressed in period clothing opened the door and told them the museum was closed. The next day, they called the museum to verify its hours of operation and discovered that the museum had in fact been open the day they were there. They described the woman at the door to the docent on the phone, who assured them none of the museum's docents wore period clothing.

The most remarkable encounter Anthony relayed to me took place during the summer. A judge who works in the New York governor's office and is also a house-history buff came to the museum with her boyfriend and her son. She was having a great time touring the house as she made her way to Mr. Tredwell's bedroom, in which there is a closet that has many Tredwell family pictures on display. She was studying the photos intently when she noticed the smell of mothballs and heard a voice similar to that of the man on those old Pepperidge Farm commercials say: "Studying the family, eh?" She turned toward the voice to discover an elderly man standing uncomfortably close to her. He was wearing a raggedy old overcoat, which she thought was odd since it was the middle of the summer and hot outside. The man was so close to her that she could see the boils on his face. He told her stories about Mr. Joseph Brewster, who built the house and lived in it for three years before selling it to the Tredwells. He said, "I knew him very well."

The woman was fearful that the man was a crazy vagrant who had wandered into the house, and she was trying to figure out how she could get assistance. Thankfully, her boyfriend and son entered the room, and she gave them the "help me" look, but they didn't know what to make of her panicked expression. She

**The front bedroom where the ghost of Seabury Tredwell is usually seen**

then discreetly motioned and mouthed the words, "The man!" as she turned to look back at the man. He was gone. The woman, her boyfriend and her son searched the hallway where they suspected the man disappeared, but they couldn't find him. They looked for him downstairs as well, to no avail. At this point, the woman was so distressed that she wanted to find a docent and report the man, but her boyfriend convinced her not to.

As they entered the front parlor, she began to calm down. Suddenly, she saw the old man in the hall walking past the parlor entrance toward the front door. He said to her, "Come back and visit us again," and then the woman heard the front door close. She yelled to her boyfriend and son to look out the front window to see the man. They ran to the windows, which were not roped off then as they are now, but they didn't see anyone on the porch or on the sidewalk in either direction. They proceeded to the front porch to investigate. There, on the porch, the realization hit her that she had been talking with a ghost!

About six months later, this woman worked up the nerve to come back to Merchant's House and knock on the door. She explained to the docent who answered that she had been to the house six months earlier. She asked the docent, "Do you ever have strange things happen here?" The docent replied, "Do you mean ghosts? Did you see a woman or a man?"

The docent took the woman to the office and showed her some family pictures, hoping she could identify who she saw. She identified Samuel Lennox Tredwell, although he appeared younger in the photograph than as the ghost she had seen. Samuel was the second-born son who didn't amount to much and was disinherited by the family.

The three main spirit sightings that Anthony noted are Gertrude, Samuel, and Seabury Tredwell. Seabury is typically spotted upstairs in or near the front bedroom. Gertrude appears in various spots, but always as a frail, petite woman, and Samuel appears as the old man the judge saw. During the holidays or special events, the activity increases, along with minor annoyances such as lights turning on by themselves and doors unlocking.

Anthony said that a couple of years ago, there was a ghost tour during Halloween. During the tour, the death of Seabury in his bedroom was reenacted, with a "dead Seabury" mannequin lying in his bed. His wake was to be staged in the front parlor. Actors had been hired to play Eliza, Gertrude, Samuel, and the servant Bridgette Murphy. It was a mini-production designed not only to entertain but also to educate the public about the life and customs of the period. As the servant reenactors maintained a steady flow of food and drink from the kitchen for the grieving family and their visitors, Bridgette talked about what servant life was like at the time. The actress playing Bridgette got laughs when she stated that she could not feel such sorrow for this dead Protestant, as she was a Catholic.

At the conclusion of the tours, Anthony was making his rounds through the museum to turn off the lights, extinguish candles, and lock up. He heard a woman humming in the back parlor which the actors had used as a dressing room. Anthony thought it was one of the actresses changing out of her costume. He was impressed by how well she "stayed in character," as she was humming a tune reminiscent of the time period. Anthony knocked on the door to inquire if she needed anything. There was no answer. He waited a couple of minutes but still heard nothing. Finally, he opened the door to find the room dark and empty. The actresses, as he confirmed later, had already left.

I visited the Merchant's House Museum on April 26, 2009. As I entered the foyer, a large tour group came down the main staircase. I made my way through the crowd and proceeded upstairs. There was only one other woman upstairs when I walked into the second bedroom on the right. She and I exchanged greetings, and I was certain she was not a ghost given her modern appearance. I went through the various rooms, examining the displays and photographs. I took pictures as my digital audio recorder recorded discreetly in my pocket. I noticed that the staircase to the third floor was roped off. I admit I was tempted to sneak up there, but I refrained. I was drawn back to Gertrude's bedroom and lingered there a while longer, hoping to catch a glimpse of her or possibly an EVP.

I went downstairs toward the back of the house to a little room that served as the gift shop. There, I spoke with a docent about the various ghostly pictures that had been turned in by ghost-tour participants over the years. The docent had not experienced any paranormal activity in her time working at the museum, but she told me that on several occasions the neighbors across the street have reported a strange light coming from the upstairs bedroom windows. The docent said that was strange indeed, because the windows have wooden shutters on the inside that are always kept closed.

After my conversation with the docent, I went to the back parlor. I was taking pictures, without flash as requested by museum personnel. I didn't capture anything unusual in those photos; however, when I attempted to take pictures in the front parlor, the camera would not cooperate. The battery level indicator showed a fully charged battery, yet the camera kept shutting down as if the battery were completely drained. Outdoors, the camera functioned perfectly again, allowing me to take pictures of the Merchant's House from across the street.

I reviewed my audio recording and confirmed that no EVPs were captured, although conditions were less than optimal given the noise from the tour group. I experienced no temperature drops (which I would have welcomed, as it was an unusually hot day in April). The photos were absent of paranormal anomalies, yet I did have that bizarre camera malfunction in the front parlor. In my interview with Anthony, he mentioned that a paranormal investigative group he chaperoned at the museum captured an EVP of footsteps on the second floor when they were all present and accounted for on the first floor. Were they the footsteps of Seabury Tredwell? Was Gertrude interfering with my camera? Maybe Samuel will be your tour guide when you visit the Merchant's House.

# CHAPTER 20

# Morris-Jumel Mansion

THE OLDEST HOUSE, and possibly the most haunted one, in New York City is the Morris-Jumel Mansion, located in the Washington Heights section of Manhattan. Even in broad daylight, the cobblestones of Jumel Terrace and the view of the Harlem River from the mansion's property set the right mood for a historic and haunted expedition.

The mansion was built in the summer of 1765 by Col. Roger Morris of the British Army. He named it Mount Morris and lived there until the outbreak of the Revolutionary War, at which time he returned to England for his own safety. The mansion was General Washington's headquarters during the Battle of Harlem Heights. Subsequent to Washington's departure, the British and the Hessians used the mansion as their base of operations during the Revolutionary War. After the war, the mansion became Calumet Hall, a stagecoach stop and tavern.

In 1810, Eliza Jumel (née Betsy Bowen) convinced her husband, a native of France and a wine merchant, to purchase the run-down mansion. Eliza and Stephen Jumel renovated the ailing mansion and decorated it in French Empire style. Stephen's wealth accrued, yet Eliza was snubbed by the high-society circles. She had been born the illegitimate daughter of a prostitute from Rhode Island, a blemish no amount of money could remove. In 1815, the Jumels visited France, returning to their mansion in New York City in 1826. Stephen died six years later.

Before I tell you about Stephen's death, I need to fast-forward to January 11, 1964. A group of schoolchildren arrived at the Morris-Jumel Mansion that morning to take a tour. The children played on the front lawn as they waited for the gardener to arrive and unlock the place. A woman came out on the balcony above the front door and yelled at the children to be quiet. "She sort of glided back into the house," one of the students said when questioned, affirming that the doors had remained closed and the woman had passed through them. The children described a tall, gray-haired lady in a faded gown. It was unmistakably Mme. Eliza Jumel. Eight days after the schoolchildren's visit, Dr. Hans Holzer brought psychic medium Ethel Meyers to the mansion to investigate the apparition. Ethel supposedly channeled the spirit of Stephen Jumel, whose spirit claimed that a boy had pushed him from a hay wagon and he had fallen onto a pitchfork. The spirit went on to say that his wife and her lover, Aaron Burr, buried him while he was still alive.

Back to 1832, when Stephen died: Some speculated that Eliza had stabbed her husband purposely with the pitchfork, while others thought he had impaled himself accidentally but that Eliza had removed the bandages too soon, causing blood loss, infection, and ultimately death. In any event, Eliza was not bereaved for very long, and in 1833 she married former Vice President Aaron Burr. Three years later, she accused Burr of cheating on her and petitioned for divorce, which was granted, ironically, the day Burr died: September 14, 1836.

My sons and I visited the Morris-Jumel Mansion four days after the forty-sixth anniversary of Holzer's investigation. It was a cold yet clear and sunny day. We knocked on the door, and Barbara, the docent on duty, answered and let us in. We paid our self-guided tour fees, and she proceeded to task my younger son, Trent, with three questions that she said she would quiz him on at the completion of our visit. Brian, my older son, was on digital-video detail; I was handling digital photography. Trent was in charge of digital audio until he got bored after five minutes, and then that became my task as well. We started downstairs in the kitchen and worked our way up to the second floor to the bedrooms.

In the hallway on the second floor is a portrait of Eliza Jumel and her two grandchildren that was painted while she and her grandchildren vacationed in Europe. Eliza was eighty years old at the time of this trip, but you would never know it from this portrait: in the painting, she has no wrinkles on her face or hands, and her eyes are clear and blue. I said aloud: "Come on, Eliza! You didn't really look like this at eighty years old. Your artist Photoshopped you!" I was hoping this would provoke Eliza's spirit to respond as an EVP while I had my audio recorder running. It didn't.

As I recorded, I was careful to note extraneous noises such as the hiss from the radiator or the sound of Brian's coat sleeve grazing the microphone as he passed by me. Therefore, I believe the whisper I captured on audio is a genuine EVP. I was standing alone in the small hallway that connects Mme. Jumel's bedroom to her dressing room. In French, I asked for Stephen Jumel to speak with me. Shortly after I said, *"Monsieur Jumel, parlez avec moi, s'il vous plait,"* a whispered response is heard in the recording. The first part of the whisper I cannot decipher at all, but the second part sounds like *"je vous aime,"* which translates as "I like you." I can attest that I did not hear this until I was home reviewing the recordings in order to write this chapter.

We returned to the first floor to inspect the front parlor, where Mme. Jumel married Aaron Burr, as well as the dining room and the octagon room. Once we finished looking around, Trent was prepared to give his answers to Barbara. Trent successfully answered all three questions and was rewarded with a goody bag filled with tokens from the mansion's gift shop. This gave me an opportunity to interview Barbara; after all, she's the one who mentioned ghosts the minute she opened the door to let us in.

Barbara has worked at the mansion since 1979. She said male visitors accompanied by a lady have reported hearing a woman's voice speaking to them from the grandfather clock. Conversely, unaccompanied men don't even notice the grandfather clock. Barbara admits that she didn't take notice until about a dozen men said the same thing. She estimates she's heard this story from sixty-two men so far.

Another interesting tale Barbara shared was of a young woman who worked part-time at the mansion. She was sitting in the foyer on a folding chair, balancing the chair on its two back legs so she could rock back and forth. She was enjoying a piece of licorice, and the grandfather clock was about five feet to her right. Suddenly, the clock began to shake and its door flung open. A voice emanating from the clock said, "You're not suitable to be in this house. Get out!" The young woman left so quickly that she didn't even grab her coat. Barbara never saw her again.

We thanked Barbara for her time and insights as we prepared to leave. Once outside, I asked my sons to make some noise. Side note for parents: This is the best way to get your children to be quiet. They both stared at me like deer mesmerized by headlights. I explained to them that I wanted to see if we could recreate the scene in which Mme. Jumel had come out onto the balcony to silence noisy children. Unfortunately, the experiment did not yield the desired results, and I ended up playing referee to separate them.

We went to the backyard of the mansion, where there is a garden. It was not in bloom at the time of our visit, but it was marked off in sections as to which plants were for cooking, which were for perfumes, and which were medicinal. We continued around the side of the house, taking pictures and videotaping. As soon as we arrived home, Brian finalized the DVD so we could review it, and I looked at my digital pictures on the computer. We captured nothing paranormal in either of those media. However, the EVP captured on the digital audio recorder sends a chill up my spine. Was it the voice of Stephen Jumel trying to communicate with me? Was he whispering because he was afraid Eliza would hear him? My advice: Brush up on your French before you visit the Morris-Jumel Mansion, and see if you can collect some EVPs. *Bonne chance!*

# Parks

# CHAPTER 21

# Fort Wadsworth

FORT WADSWORTH, ON STATEN ISLAND, stands just below the Verrazano-Narrows Bridge. It comprises Battery Weed, positioned along the shore, and Fort Tompkins, which was set higher up for a better vantage point out to sea before the bridge was built. Fort Wadsworth was constructed in 1824 to protect New York City, along with its sister fort, Fort Hamilton in Brooklyn. The two forts face each other, creating a gateway between the Atlantic Ocean and the Hudson River. Battery Weed is named for Brigadier General Steven Weed, who died during the battle at Gettysburg in 1864. Since 1997, Fort Wadsworth has been part of the National Parks Service.

Tours of the fortification emphasize its historical and architectural value. Visitors walk through the catacomb-like passageways, the dry moat, and the parade area, and they get to step inside the former powder magazine.

Lynda Lee Macken, author of *Haunted History of Staten Island*, writes that "[i]ndividuals have shared that while enjoying the vista they heard gun shots. Then they saw an agitated mob of elders carrying lanterns up the hill from the beach. The pack marched silently past the visitors as if they were invisible. As the phantoms continued on their way they simply vanished." On the *Haunted Places in Staten Island* Web site, the following report was made: "The ghosts here like to play games with the eyes. A ghost of a mysterious soldier has been seen walking through walls, and moving cars. Some people have also reported blacking out and having flashbacks. One woman reported flashing back to war time and seeing through the eyes of a nurse with black curly hair. She saw people hurt and dying in a room. When she looked outside a window, a soldier grabbed her arm and turned her around, screaming in her ear, telling her to get down and take cover. The room exploded and she came back to reality. Also, within a blink of the eye, one could see dead soldiers with blood on an empty field."

I've been visiting Fort Wadsworth since 2002 and have taken my sons there for the Fourth of July fireworks. The Fort is a great venue for fireworks; I figured it had to be a great venue for the paranormal as well, based on its age and its close proximity to the water. I've noticed over my years of paranormal investigating that water seems to amplify ghostly activity. In haunted houses, I've investigated, activity has been greatest in the kitchen, the bathroom, or the rooms that adjoin kitchen or bathroom plumbing. The water acts like a conduit for the ghost, helping it to manifest. Haunted properties are usually close by water, such as a lake, river, or ocean. For example, both Conference House and the Alice Austen house sit on the waterfront.

In April, 2010, my sons and I visited Fort Wadsworth to investigate it. We arrived ahead of the tour time to wander through the exhibits at the Visitor's Center and watch the ten-minute movie about the history of the fort. From there, we went outside to explore on our own. The Verrazano-Narrows Bridge was obscured by a thick fog. I was hopeful that we'd have some paranormal activity while on the tour, as fog is another atmospheric condition that magnifies ghostly manifestations.

Tours are free at Fort Wadsworth, and the park rangers are very knowledgeable. Park ranger Justine was our tour guide. She started our tour in the parking lot. She asked us if we could see the fort behind her. We couldn't see a fort, just a small hill. That was intentional, she explained: When enemy soldiers approached, they thought they were coming upon a small hill to climb. Little did they know that on the other side was a dry moat. The soldiers would fall into the dry moat, where they were trapped with no escape as bullets fired from small openings ricocheted off the roughly cut stone walls.

We followed Justine to the parade ground of Fort Tompkins. Brian was recording video, and I was taking pictures and recording audio. It was getting much colder by this time because of the fog. Justine explained the daily routine of the 750 to 1,500 soldiers who were housed inside the fort at any given time. She took us to what used to be the mess hall. I took some pictures there and continued to record. One picture yielded a couple of orbs, but I wrote them off as resulting from the moisture of the place. I collected no EVPs there.

We went back out to the parade ground. Brian let out an exasperated sigh and said, "I can't believe this." I turned around to ask him what was wrong. He told me the battery on the camcorder was dying, showing me the low-battery symbol flashing on the view screen. We knew we had charged the camera before we left home and that we had 319 minutes of power when

The catacombs at Fort Wadsworth

we arrived at Fort Wadsworth. I told Brian to keep recording until the camcorder died completely. I wanted to see if the battery power would regain strength, as had happened once when I was investigating the Bloody Chapel of Leap Castle in Ireland. Unfortunately, the camcorder powered down within minutes. Fortunately, my digital audio recorder and camera retained their battery life, so I was able to document the rest of the tour.

After the tour, I asked Ranger Justine if she had ever encountered ghosts while working at the fort. She said she hadn't personally, but she knew there was a relevant book on sale at the visitors' center, and she suggested that one of the rangers there might have something more to share. Sure enough, they had the book by Lynda Lee Macken. I grabbed it and, while paying for it, asked the ranger if he had any paranormal experiences to share regarding the fort. He said he vaguely remembered a story of a tragic incident that happened on the parade ground pre-World War I, but he wasn't sure of the details. He referred me to Dan

Meharg, a park ranger stationed at Sandy Hook, New Jersey, who had once worked at Fort Wadsworth.

I contacted Dan, and he was exceptionally helpful. He had suspicions about the energy of Fort Wadsworth while he was stationed there, and he had researched the subject online via newspaper articles from the *New York Tribune* and the *New York Times*. One of the stories he sent me gave me chills. In September of 1920, the Red Cross brought 960 Russian children from Siberia to Fort Wadsworth to live until they could be returned to their parents by way of France. While the children were at the fort, some of them attempted to escape. The first time, approximately one hundred boys escaped, fifty of whom were caught and brought back to the fort. The second time, seventy-five boys escaped and only fifteen were recaptured. Perhaps the eerie vision of a lantern-toting mob that disappears is a residual haunting of the people who were looking for these escaped Russian boys.

On the morning of September 10, 1920, some soldiers at the fort had just finished their morning rifle demonstrations. As reported in the *New York Times*:

> *Pavel Nikolovff, 14 years old, was killed in the morning when Private John Burhim was demonstrating with his rifle. The bullet entered the little fellow's head. The boy, with a stick of wood on his shoulder for a rifle, met the soldier returning from guard duty and marched with him. Nearly forty other boys, as well as Red Cross nurses, physicians, and officials, laughingly watched the soldier and little Pavel. As Burhim was about to place his rifle on the rack they saw the little fellow go through the Russian manual of arms. When the boy finished the evolutions, the soldier picked up his rifle again to show the lad the difference between the Russian and the American manual. As he was bringing the rifle to "present," one of his fingers struck the trigger. Burhim caught the*

*falling boy in his arms and ran to the Post Hospital where it was discovered Pavel had been instantly killed.*

Ultimately the event was declared an accident.

This sad and traumatic event would explain the battery drain on the camcorder my nineteen-year-old son was using. I think the spirit of this fourteen-year-old Russian boy was drawn to Brian because Brian is around the age Private Burhim probably was at the time of the accidental shooting. We were, in a way, "marching" up the parade ground as we toured it. The little spirit may have interpreted the camcorder in Brian's hands as a rifle.

Dan said he hopes that the park will eventually open Battery Weed for tours. He told me about a deadly explosion at the battery in 1890. A cartridge shell exploded for reasons unknown, igniting thirty-five pounds of gunpowder in one of the casements. The explosion claimed the life of Nathaniel Chapman and severely burned several others. It's possible that a ghostly soldier seen walking through walls and among cars may be the spirit of Chapman. Or it could be the spirit of Louis Bauer, a twenty-four-year-old who shot and killed himself on October 11, 1891, at Fort Wadsworth. Bauer had feelings for another man's wife, a Mrs. Grube. She was able to converse with him in German as they were from the same town in Germany, and he developed feelings for her. Because she was married, she didn't reply to the letters he wrote to her. Apparently the unrequited love was more than he could bear. She did, however, claim his body and arrange for a proper burial.

While no battles were fought at Fort Wadsworth, a battle reenactment here on June 19, 1908, resulted in three men being killed during a "sham bay fight." The backfire explosion of a six-inch gun at Battery Dix thrust one man into the wall, crushing his skull. The second casualty had an arm blown off and was severely burned, while the third man's cause of death was undetermined. A Catholic priest was called and arrived in time to administer the Last Rites to these three men. Perhaps those tragic mock battles account for the ghostly gunfire heard at the fort to this day.

These tragic events may explain the ghostly sightings and paranormal activity that have been reported at Fort Wadsworth. Although most of the park rangers will not discuss such matters, you now know what to look for while enjoying the tour. I did get a chuckle out of the fact that a Fort Wadsworth park ranger told me the "ghosty stuff" happens at the Statue of Liberty, while a Statue of Liberty park ranger said "that stuff" happens at Fort Wadsworth. Either way, history and tragedy have combined at Fort Wadsworth to create a haunting worthy of exploration.

# CHAPTER 22

# Washington Square Park

TODAY, A STROLL THROUGH Washington Square Park is relaxing. There is a small playground for children, a beautiful arched monument with President Washington's statue on it, and plenty of benches on which to rest. After my friends and I graduated from high school, most Friday nights involved a late-night run to "the city" to meet and hang out at Washington Square Park. (In fact, until I visited the park for this book project, I had never been there in daylight.) It was a hip place to be, given its proximity to New York University (NYU). I was always the only female in the group, which consisted of my then-fiancé and all his friends. Additionally, I was always the designated driver— except for the time the guys forgot I hadn't yet learned to drive a car with a manual transmission. Yes, that was a frightening ride home in Dave's tiny Opal! Needless to say, after that my then-fiancé made it his mission to teach me to drive a stick-shift.

Back then, I had no idea that the very park I was hanging in was so macabre. If you recall the climax of the movie *Poltergeist,* when the father realizes that only the headstones were moved and not the bodies, then you have a clear picture of what lies beneath this seemingly pleasant park. As long ago as 1793, Washington Square Park was a potter's field (a cemetery for the poor) where Leni-Lenape Indians who had succumbed to yellow fever were buried. During the 1800s, the rate of burials quickened due to a cholera epidemic. Bodies were supposed to be buried eight to thirteen feet below ground, but as the gravediggers' backlog of work grew, they got sloppy, digging some graves as shallow as three feet. The problem became evident when the potter's field was converted to a parade ground in 1826. The weight of parading artillery caused the shallow graves to collapse, leaving the artillery stuck in morbid potholes. By 1828, the area had become a simple park, albeit one with almost 20,000 bodies under it.

That history might explain the chains that cordon off expansive areas of lawn in Washington Square Park, punctuated at intervals with signs that read: "Passive Lawn, No Sports, No Dogs." (The first I noticed those signs, I chuckled to myself, wondering what an aggressive lawn would look like.) Of course, dogs love to dig, so a boneyard of this capacity would have every canine in the city tearing at its earth. I can imagine, too, that playing sports such as football would be dangerous if one were tackled atop a protruding bone fragment.

In the northwest corner of the park, near Green Street and Washington Place, is an old English elm tree that once was a hanging tree. With its massive trunk seventy-six inches in diameter, the tree has an eerie appearance even in broad daylight. The last person to be hanged publicly from this tree was Rose Butler, a domestic servant, on July 8, 1819. Rose was condemned for starting a fire in the house where she worked. It's said that she never confessed to the supposed crime, and that, in all likelihood, the fire started by accident. Reports persist to this day of a shadowy body seen swinging in the breeze late at night from the branches of this tree.

While at the park, I met two New York City police officers standing by the former hanging tree. I asked them if they had ever noticed anything weird or unsettling about the park. One officer replied, "Beyond the everyday weird and strange that is New York City? No." He did point out the hanging tree behind us, and he knew 1819 was the year of the last hanging there.

There is another historical event dealing with fire that took place in this same northwest area of the park. It was a tragic fire on March 25, 1911, that took the lives of 146 people, mostly girls and women ages thirteen to twenty-three. Today the building involved in the fire is known as the Frederick Brown Building of New York University, and it houses office space and some classrooms. In 1911, it was the Asch Building, and the Triangle Shirtwaist Factory occupied the top three of its ten stories. It is believed that the blaze started when a smoldering cigarette butt or match was thrown on the floor, which was littered with fabric scraps. The workers attempted to extinguish the fire themselves, but it quickly grew out of control. Horrifically, the girls and women were trapped in the building because the doors of the factory were locked—supposedly to prevent theft of the precious bolts of fabric, although some say it was to prevent workers from leaving early. The sad fact remains that the managers who had the keys to the locked doors exited the building at the first sign of smoke. Some workers tried the fire escape, but it collapsed from the weight of so many people on it at one time. Others made it out of the building via the elevator: its normal capacity was ten people, but almost twice that many managed to cram into the elevator and reach the ground, their clothes burned from their bodies. Some workers were so desperate to escape that they tried to shinny down the elevator cables, only to fall on top of the elevator and die. The elevator operator, Joe Zitto, said blood dripped on him from above and he heard change falling from the pockets of those atop the elevator.

The few doors that were unlocked opened inward instead of outward as is required today. Hysterical workers piled up at those doors, crushing them closed as they burned to death. Charred bodies of women who jumped to their deaths piled up so quickly beside the building that the fire companies on the scene were unable to get close enough to the building to fight the fire. Even after room was made for a fire truck, the ladders and hoses reached only to the sixth floor. The adjacent Brown Building, occupied by the NYU law department, was twelve feet taller than the Asch building. Students there rigged together two ladders and lowered them to the roof of the burning building, and approximately 150 workers made the harrowing trip up the ladders to safety.

The lives of 146 women and girls were lost in this fire. The tragedy resulted in new labor laws and fire codes that required doors to open outward and to be kept unlocked during working hours.

In the magical arts, fire is believed to purify. Incense is burned, for example, to cleanse and sanctify an altar space. By contrast, a fire resulting in the tragic loss of so many lives is not so purifying and cleansing. Even today, NYU students taking classes in the Brown Building say they feel as if they're suffocating and have the overwhelming desire to get out of the building and catch their breath.

Another building at NYU, the Bobst Library, has a sad history: it is known not just for its for its stunning architectural design, but also for suicides who jump from upper floors of the library into the atrium below. The pattern of the floor in the atrium resembles spikes when viewed from above, but this has not discouraged jumpers as intended. Twenty-year-old John Skolnik jumped to his death on September 12, 2003. Stephen Bohler, 18, did the same on October 10, 2003, although Bohler's death was ruled an accident due to the presence of drugs in his bloodstream. By October 14, 2003, NYU announced it would install glass walls as barriers to prevent future suicide attempts. There were other NYU student suicides in 2004 and 2005, but they did not occur in the library. The barriers worked until November 3, 2009, when Andrew Williamson-Noble, 20, managed to jump to his death in the library at 4:30 A.M.

At first I wondered if the students who died at Bobst Library were somehow haunted by the 1911 Triangle Shirtwaist fire and were perhaps reenacting the fatal jumps of the factory women. However, the library is at the opposite end of Washington Square from the factory. I also researched whether any of these students might have taken classes in the Brown Building next to the factory, but only one had that I could determine.

I spoke with Spencer S., an NYU student, who told me the Brittany Residence Hall is known to be haunted. He said the ghost is that of the girl who threw herself down the elevator shaft there. I didn't find any news articles to confirm that story, but I did find other interesting information about this dormitory. Located at 55 East Tenth Street, this residence hall was originally the Brittany Hotel, built in 1929. The hotel's penthouse, which today is the student lounge, was a speakeasy during Prohibition. Strange music and disembodied footsteps are reported there, as are mysterious lights and a feeling of being watched. Perhaps the ghost of one-time hotel guest Jerry Garcia, of the Grateful Dead, is keeping an eye on things.

Unless you're a student at NYU or know someone who is, you cannot enter the Brown Building. However, there is plenty for the paranormal investigator to explore at Washington Square Park and its hanging tree. Collecting EVPs in a park is challenging; still, it might be worth hanging around the hanging tree with your digital audio recorder in hand. With close to 20,000 bodies buried in the park, along with the site of the tragic Triangle Shirtwaist fire nearby, you have a pretty good chance of capturing a disembodied scream or moan.

# Cemeteries

# CHAPTER 23

# Woodlawn Cemetery

WOODLAWN CEMETERY IN THE BRONX was founded in 1863. Its 400 acres are easily accessible from Manhattan via trains from Grand Central Station, as well as by car using the Major Deegan (I-87) or I-95. The intention behind the location was to have a peaceful place away from the downtown noise, but not too far away. The original design of the cemetery was based on the "rural cemetery movement" that originated in 1831 with Mount Auburn Cemetery in Boston. However, five years after the cemetery opened, its design was changed to a "landscape lawn plan," which prohibited fences and encouraged central monuments with footstones. The cleaner, more spacious grounds made cemetery maintenance much easier.

A few of the 300,000 people interred at Woodlawn are mentioned in this book—people such as the Van Cortlandts, Herman Melville, and Olive Thomas Pickford. Other famous people buried there include George M. Cohan, Fiorello Henry LaGuardia, Nellie Bly, Joseph Pulitzer, and Thomas Nast. For those of you who appreciate retail shopping, F.W. Woolworth, Roland H. Macy, and James Cash Penney are buried there, too. Woodlawn offers many free events, such as concerts, walking and bus tours, theater performances, and a tree lighting during the holidays. It's more than a cemetery; it's a cultural resource for the Bronx.

Photography is allowed in the cemetery as long as you stop by the office upon arrival, present a photo ID, and complete a simple form. I recommend you follow the formal steps in case you capture some amazing paranormal evidence and want to

Woodlawn Cemetery is full of famous people, including the former mayor of New York.

share it on your Web site or in a newspaper article. The cemetery grounds are open every day from 8:30 A.M. to 5 P.M., but the office, where photography permission is secured, is closed on Sundays.

When I first visited Woodlawn, the ground was snow-covered and it was difficult to walk around; some of the drifts were more than three feet high. So I went back in early March of 2010 with Dina Chirico, my team leader at the New Jersey Ghost Hunters Society. Dina is a great navigator, which helped tremendously; she read the map and directed me while I drove. The first grave I was determined to find was that of Herman Melville. What writer could refuse the chance to pay respects to one of the greats? I certainly couldn't.

According to the map, Melville's grave was located in the Catalpa section of the cemetery. We drove over to it and parked.

**Herman Melville's grave**

Dina and I employed a "divide and conquer" strategy to find the grave: she started at one end of the section, and I went to the other. I had my digital audio recorder running the whole time I was searching. I noted on the recording the date, time, and weather; I also took some photos while searching.

As I started up a small incline, I saw what appeared to be a baby's grave. I said into my recorder, "a little . . . it looks like a little baby grave. Born January 2, 1871, died . . . I can't make out the month . . . seventeenth of 1872." When I reviewed the recording, right after I said, "looks like a little baby grave," I heard the voice of a woman whisper, "Yeah." I know it's not my voice because I was speaking at a normal conversational volume, and the EVP interjects so closely after my previous word, it's impossible that I could have said it. I know it's not Dina's voice, either; she was so far away from me at the time that she had to yell to ask if I had found Melville's grave yet. I shut the recorder off so I could yell back to her that I hadn't. I didn't know I had captured an EVP until I got home and reviewed the recording.

Dina and I reconvened at my car and reviewed the map once more. She knew we were close to Melville's grave, and she became even more determined to find it. We started out again, and Dina found it. Honestly, I was expecting a huge monument for someone like him, but it was a simple, modest headstone. Little rocks and trinkets left by previous visitors sat atop the headstone. There was also a handwritten note that said, "Thanks. You changed my life."

Dina and I waited quietly around Melville's grave for a bit, recording for EVPs. Then we left to find LaGuardia's grave. Fiorello LaGuardia was mayor of New York City from 1934 to 1945. He was a short, rotund man with a high-pitched voice, but full of fire and conviction. He did not like the shame and negative stereotypes the mob had brought to Italian culture. LaGuardia put it best when he said, "Let's drive the bums out of town." He had Lucky Luciano arrested, and he went after Frank Costello's slot machines with a sledgehammer. It was a media event when the slot machines were dumped onto a barge to be taken away from New York City.

Dina and I found LaGuardia's grave much more easily than Melville's. By then it was getting late, and we couldn't hang around to conduct an EVP session. Dina took some pictures of the grave before we left the cemetery.

Judging by how effortlessly I captured an EVP while walking around Woodlawn Cemetery, I am sure there are more to be found on a return trip. I wonder what Joseph Pulitzer, "father of journalism," has to say these days.

# Spotlight: Hart Island

To the east of City Island in the Bronx is Hart Island. Originally purchased by Thomas Pell from the Siwanoy Indians in 1654, Hart Island is uninhabited and serves as a potter's field, a cemetery for indigent or unidentified dead. It is estimated that 800,000 unidentified bodies, stacked three deep per grave, are buried within the cemetery's 101 acres. Ironically, prisoners at Riker's Island consider the task of gravedigging on Hart Island the best job to volunteer for. They like being out of Riker's for the day, enjoying the fresh air on the ferry to Hart Island. The inmates on this detail refer to themselves as the "death patrol" or "potter's navy."

During the Civil War, Union troops trained at Hart Island and created the first cemetery for their fallen soldiers there. Later in the war, the island served as a prison for captured Confederate soldiers; 235 Confederates died there and were buried in unmarked graves.

The first civilian burial on the island was Louisa Van Slyke, a twenty-four-year-old orphan, in 1869. Around that time, the former military barracks were converted to workhouses for delinquent boys. In 1925, Solomon Riley constructed two hundred feet of boardwalk with bath houses and a dance hall, intending to create an amusement park for the blacks of Harlem, who were barred from other such parks. Riley's vision was never realized; he was forced to sell his four acres because city officials thought his recreation area would corrupt the "reformatory environment." Riley's attempted resort was torn down.

Several buildings operated on the island during World War II. One served as a quarantine hospital for sufferers of highly contagious diseases such as tuberculosis and yellow fever. Another was a reform school and a naval disciplinary barracks. Once, the captured crew of a

German U-boat were held at Hart Island. In 1955, the Army constructed a Nike missile base on the island; it was rendered obsolete by 1961. The rusting remnants of missile silos, along with their sealed ventilation shafts, serve today as reminders of the Cold War.

Author Melinda Hunt and photographer Joel Sternfeld collaborated to produce the book *Hart Island.* They visited Hart Island on November 7, 2008. Melinda writes that they found "a solitary grave" that was the resting place of the first child victim of AIDS to be buried on the island. She continued:

> *Extra precautions were taken to bury the child in a separate and deeper grave. The forested isolation of this grave reminded me that this part of the island had also been used as quarantine for yellow fever. The yellow fever burials at Madison Square Park and Washington Square had also been individual graves. This AIDS grave seemed like a tomb to an unknown child. It came to represent all children who were yet to die of AIDS as well as child victims of earlier epidemics. This burial was the essence of a potter's field: a removed landscape where the fearsome, the lonely and the unknown are buried out of sight.*

An eerie energy permeates Hart Island to this day. It is desolate, with abandoned buildings and overgrown walkways. Old shoes are strewn about, leftovers from the days of a drug rehabilitation program called Phoenix House where leatherworking was a form of rehabilitative therapy for patients. Few people get to visit Hart Island; those who do must go through the proper channels of the New York City Department of Corrections.

For any of you who might want to venture to Hart Island without obtaining the proper permission, let January 24, 2003, serve as a warning. On that date, four young men—Charles Wertenbaker, 16; Andrew Melnikov, 16; Max Guarino, 17; and Henry Badillo, 17—were at a party on City Island. They left the party at approximately 9:30 P.M. with a plan to "borrow" a rowboat from Barron's Marina and head to Hart Island. Just before 10 p.m, Henry Badillo placed a call to 911 from his cell phone. He told the dispatcher that they were in the Long Island Sound and their boat was taking on water. Unfortunately, the call cut out after only twelve seconds. The dispatcher entered "Long Island Sound" into her computer system, and nothing came up for that location, so she approached her supervisor for advice on how best to proceed. The supervisor decided too little information was available and therefore did nothing. Fourteen hours later, when the parents of one of the boys reported their son missing, the U.S. Coast Guard began its search. Realistically, the boys had little chance of being rescued after being subjected to the freezing water for that amount of time. Nine days later, on February 2, a battered fiberglass boat was found thirty feet off the coast of Hart Island. A wrapper from an apple turnover was found floating under the capsized boat; it was determined to be from the Sunoco gas station and convenience store at which the boys were last seen. Over the next four months, all four bodies were eventually recovered.

The grim environment of Hart Island has been an inspiration for Hollywood. A movie entitled *Don't Say a Word* starring Michael Douglas featured a final scene filmed on Hart Island. The man-eating-flies horror film *Island of the Dead* was also filmed on the island.

Surprisingly, Academy Award–winning child star Bobby Driscoll is buried on Hart Island. He died in 1968 at the age of 31 of advanced hardening of the arteries from extensive drug use. His body was found in a tenement in the East Village, but his identity was unknown, so he was buried on Hart Island. Almost two years later, his mother initiated a search for her long-lost son in the hopes of facilitating a reunion between him and his father, who was near death. A fingerprint match at the NYPD confirmed that Bobby's remains were on Hart Island. Mrs. Driscoll opted to place a memorial plaque for her son at the cemetery next to her husband's grave, as it was cheaper than disinterring Bobby's body and shipping it to the other cemetery.

A tour of Hart Island is held annually on Ascension Thursday. I plan on attending this year's tour. Unfortunately, it will take place well after this book is printed. Keep an eye on the *America's Haunted Road Trip* Web site (www.americashauntedroadtrip.com) where I will be adding a detailed blog of my experience on Hart Island.

Hart Island is under the direction and control of the New York City Department of Corrections and therefore photography is not permitted—not even on the pier on City Island, from which the annual Ascension Thursday tour departs. So, while it would be impossible to conduct a formal paranormal investigation there, ghosthunters would be remiss to pass up a chance to at least visit. Clay Risen of *The Morning News* summed it up best: "Those who have been to Hart Island invariably refer to it as 'lonely' and 'creepy,' an island so full of the dead that it has, itself, ceased to exist in any real sense. Prisoners arrive, bury their daily load, and then leave quickly; no one stays very long. They hurry back to City Island, where, standing on the shore, you can still feel the loneliness, wafting across the water."

# Spotlight: How to Conduct a Cemetery Ghost Hunt

A cemetery is a great place to do some training for new members of your ghosthunting group and to practice using new equipment. The New Jersey Ghost Hunter's Society conducts cemetery hunts from spring to early fall. New members are required to participate in two cemetery hunts, working alongside team leaders for hands-on training. After that, new members are eligible to participate in a paranormal investigation at a client home or place of business.

Some people maintain that cemeteries simply are not haunted. I disagree. Members of my local group have witnessed a full-body apparition of a man in a turn-of-the-century butler's uniform dusting off his tombstone. I don't believe that every ghost hangs around his or her grave. I think some spirits return to the place where they died or where they were most happy in life, while others actually "cross over." I also think that sometimes a spirit that has crossed over can come back to Earth to see who's at their grave or to intervene on a loved one's behalf, then return to wherever it is they normally reside.

Many NJGHS members have captured EVPs during cemetery hunts. I will concede, however, that the old cemeteries and graveyards from the Revolutionary War period are *dead*. I have had better success in more recent cemeteries dating from 1900s.

Just to clarify, there is a difference between a cemetery and a graveyard. Cemeteries are stand-alone properties, whereas graveyards are on church property. Again, I find the pre–Civil War graveyards to be void of paranormal activity.

To conduct a cemetery hunt, it's best to scope out your location in the daytime first. Get a lay of the land and take note of any "No Trespassing" signs. Obviously if signs state "No Trespassing,"

"No Visiting After Dusk," or "No Visitors After 8 P.M.," you should pick another cemetery, unless you're able to gain permission that supersedes the posted rules. Also, decide ahead of time which areas of the cemetery you will assign team members to investigate, and map any open graves to prevent a teammate from falling in.

If you can find the caretaker on site, speak with him directly about setting up a night when your group can visit and take some readings. If you can't find the caretaker, you'll have to find the number of the cemetery's main office or, in the case of a Catholic cemetery, the church's monsignor. When you call, explain that your group is interested in the cemetery's historical value and that you will conduct your investigation with reverence and scientific professionalism. The NJGHS, for example, strictly prohibits smoking, drinking, and eating during a cemetery hunt. This not only prevents thoughtless littering, it also allows for cleaner evidence capture. Some cemeteries will ask that you or your team leader check in at the local police department before your hunt, while others may send you a fax confirming you have permission to be there on that date and time.

To increase your chances of finding paranormal activity, try to book the cemetery hunt as close to the full moon as possible. On a clear night with a full moon, there is usually sufficient light to navigate without the constant use of a flashlight. Over the years, I've noticed better evidence results on full moon nights as opposed to other less moonlit nights. Also, hunting three to five days after a solar flare will increase your chances of success, as solar flares increase the earth's electromagnetic field. It's believed that spirits draw energy from this electromagnetic field; the stronger it is, the more easily the spirits can manifest.

Prior to your cemetery hunt, establish a safe place for participants to park their cars and convene. The NJGHS uses a sign-in sheet to register each participant so the team leader has an accurate head count. Before the hunt begins, it's best to review your investigative protocols, if your organization has them, and to set a time to reconvene. Discourage members from investigating alone; at a minimum, they should work in pairs. Cell phones should be turned off so as not to interfere with EVP work. If the cemetery is large and you have more than one team leader taking groups to specific sections, a two-way radio is best. When the hunt is over, before leaving the cemetery, the team leader is responsible for doing a head count to make sure everyone has returned.

For EVP work in a cemetery, try leaving an audio recorder on a headstone to record while you work elsewhere. Do not use voice-activated mode; simply set it to record constantly. You can also carry a recorder with you and prompt for EVPs by asking, "If there's anyone here, would you please tell me your name?" Remember to remain silent and continue recording for at least fifteen to thirty seconds after you ask the question.

For photography work in a cemetery, remember that most headstones are made of granite and therefore will reflect a lot of light from the camera's flash. You can use a flash; just don't point it directly at a headstone, and remember the flash will reach approximately eight feet in front of you. If your camera has an infrared mode that allows shooting in zero light, such as Sony's NightShot, you should use it.

Try experimenting with "familiarity vibrations" to see if you can coax spirits out to be documented. For example, paranormal investigators on the battlefields of Gettysburg play Civil War–era music to see if the spirit activity increases. If during your daytime preview of the cemetery you noticed a headstone of a dancer, you might play some music from that person's time period to see if the spirit responds or manifests.

For any significant evidence in photos, videos, or audio recordings, make note of the location, then have your team historian research the person buried in the nearest grave. For example, if you capture an EVP of a woman's voice that seems to be saying "water," but you aren't sure if you're hearing the EVP correctly, historical research could provide some confirmation if you find that the woman in the nearby grave died by drowning.

The good thing about a cemetery hunt is you can revisit and compare the results from one investigation to the next. Good luck!

# Theaters

# CHAPTER 24

# Belasco Theater

AT THE TIME OF THIS WRITING, the Belasco Theater is undergoing renovations. It is set to reopen in the fall of 2010. It will be well worth a visit to see a show here once it reopens. The theater is named after David Belasco, who was born on July 25, 1853, in San Francisco, California, to parents of Portuguese and Jewish heritage.

David Belasco was known as "the Bishop of Broadway" because he dressed in dark suits and turned his starched collar backwards to resemble a cleric's collar. It's said that he wore his collar backwards in honor of a Father McGuire who tutored him when he was a boy. However, any similarity between Belasco and a bishop or other clergyman ends with the collar, as I'll explain later on.

Belasco became involved in the theater at a young age, working as a callboy performing odd jobs. When he was only eleven years old, he made his acting debut in *Richard III*. He penned his first play, *The Regulator's Revenge*, at the age of twelve. At nineteen, Belasco became the stage manager of the Baldwin Theater in San Francisco. By 1882, Belasco had moved to New York City to work at the Madison Square Theater as stage manager. According to *The Jewish Virtual Library* (http://www.jewish-virtuallibrary.org), "In 1893, Belasco wrote his first real hit, *The Girl I Left Behind Me*. During his career between 1884 and 1930, Belasco wrote, directed, or produced more than 100 Broadway plays including *The Hearth of Maryland* (1895) and *Madame Butterfly* (1900). During the early 20th century, Belasco also began to produce the works of other writers."

For his stage sets, Belasco was obsessed by a high standard for naturalism. His attention to detail mandated that actual coffee be brewed, or pancakes cooked, to incorporate those aromas into the play at the precise time they were needed. Further to his credit, he is known for his use of innovative lighting techniques that set the mood of the play.

In 1907, Belasco built the Stuyvesant Theater, located at 111 West 44th Street in New York City. As movie houses were gaining popularity and larger audiences, Belasco wanted to create a theater that was more intimate to draw the patrons into the action of the plays. What he lacked in physical stature (he was only five feet two inches tall), he made up for with his state-of-the-art staging effects.

In 1910, Belasco renamed the Stuyvesant Theater after himself, built an elevator under part of the stage to raise and lower it, and installed a special-effects studio and an advanced lighting system. Above the theater, he constructed an apartment where he spent a great deal of his time. Despite being a married man, he auditioned up-and-coming actresses on his "casting couch" in this nest of his above the theater. (Remember, I said any similarity between Belasco and clergy ended with the collar.)

At the time of his death in 1931, Belasco had been married for fifty years, and he left behind a legacy of theater entertainment. But did he leave more? Shortly after his death, people at his theater heard footsteps when no one was there, and actors and actresses reported seeing the dark shadow of a man in the balcony while they performed on stage. On occasion, he would materialize so solidly that he could shake the hand of an actor after a performance and verbally congratulate him on a job well done. Even as a ghost, Belasco's attention to detail was evident! Sometimes his ghost would pinch the bottoms of pretty young actresses, who found this behavior extremely disturbing coming from someone dressed "like a monk." Over time, it became a good omen for an actor to encounter the ghost of David Belasco. Of course, the less experienced actors weren't so thrilled; his apparition truly frightened them.

The scent of Belasco's cigar is smelled occasionally and disappears as mysteriously as it appeared. The sounds of people laughing and partying are heard emanating from Belasco's former apartment above the theater. Theater workers have heard Belasco's private elevator going up and down between the apartment and theater in spite of the fact that the shaft has been sealed and the motor disconnected for years. An article in *Playbill* titled *The Ghosts of Broadway* reports, "Closed doors on the set have been seen to magically open in unison as the curtain rises."

A former usher at the Belasco Theater said that one night while closing up, she said aloud, "Good night, Mr. Belasco." No sooner did she finish saying the words than all the lobby doors swung wide open. After that, this usher refused to work there ever again.

Belasco enjoyed the company of women while he was alive, and he continues such enjoyment even in death. A ghostly red-headed woman in a negligee has been seen over the years in the theater. It's thought that she is the ghost of a red-haired stripper who hanged herself in the basement of the theater years ago. And no ghost production would be complete without the leading lady; here, it's the Blue Lady. This female apparition has been seen many times, most notably on one occasion when an actress was taking a shower in her dressing room and heard the locked door open. She grabbed a towel as she jumped out of the shower to confront the intruder, only to find the door still locked and the bathroom enveloped in a strange blue glow. In 1982, an electrician working in the theater saw a woman in a blue gown, with dark hair and fair skin, walk briskly across the back of the balcony. He said she seemed intent on getting to her destination, for she was so focused that she was completely unaware of his watching her. Later, he learned about a woman who was on her way to Belasco's apartment for a job interview but died when an elevator malfunctioned. She has been spotted in the balcony by a number of performers. Once, her blue blur ascended the stairs to Belasco's apartment without tripping the motion-sensing alarm system, while a theater employee felt the chill go by him.

It's said that Belasco's ghost sat in his private box for every premier except that of *Oh! Calcutta!* That play, which brought full frontal nudity (both male and female) to the stage, seemed to drive away Belasco's spirit. Fortunately for ghosthunters and actors seeking that good-luck sighting, Belasco's ghost returned once that show left his theater.

I have been to the Belasco twice in an effort to complete this chapter. On my first visit, I saw the scaffolding and netting covering the face of the theater and was disappointed, fearing I would have to eliminate the Belasco chapter from my book. Thanks to my mom and her "try, try again" spirit, we made a return trip.

She suggested we visit the Booth Theater, since Edwin Booth, the actor, was a contemporary of Belasco's, and she had read that the Booth Theater is haunted. Perhaps the renovations at the Belasco Theater forced Belasco's ghost to relocate to his friend's namesake theater.

Janice, at the Booth Theater, was very kind and helpful. She maintained, "Not my theater! It's not haunted." But she went on to say that the Belasco *is* haunted. She called there and arranged for Chris West, the Belasco's security manager, to meet with me.

We walked over to the Belasco Theater, and Chris buzzed in through the stage door gate. Chris has worked as security at the Belasco for three years. He said he sometimes feels a presence that he attributes to David Belasco. He went on to say, "I get here every morning around 5:15, and in the winter it's dark out still, so it's pretty creepy being here in the theater alone. I just make sure I say, 'Good morning, Mr. Belasco,' when I walk in, and that seems to set the tone to where he keeps a safe distance from me and doesn't freak me out." Chris then told me about a very recent and bizarre event. The theater's electricians, two men probably in their early twenties, were preparing the new wiring. They left two wires close together, to be joined later, while they attended to something else. When they returned, they found the wires connected. Chris said the young men were frightened by this discovery, and that they were not ones to frighten easily. I asked Chris if the recent renovations at the theater seemed to be amplifying the paranormal activity. He said he's noticed a cold spot every now and then, but nothing overwhelming or frightening. He also said that construction workers have found it challenging to keep track of their tools; they frequently put a tool down in one spot and find it on the other side of the work area when they return.

In 2008, Spike Lee filmed the final performance of *Passing Strange* at the Belasco. I'm told Spike heard about the haunted activity in the former apartment above the Belasco and wanted to check it out for himself. Chris isn't sure whether Spike found anything there, however, as he wasn't on duty that day.

As for me and my findings, I wasn't allowed in the theater during the construction for safety reasons. Chris and I conversed in the alley by the stage door. I didn't capture any EVPs or any anomalies in my digital photos, but I'm determined to go back to the Belasco in the fall of 2010 to catch a glimpse of "the Bishop of Broadway" on opening night. I have the feeling that the most haunting sequel at the Belasco is yet to be staged.

# Spotlight: Theater Superstitions and Traditions

Theaters are rich sources for paranormal phenomena. Before you venture into a theater to start hunting, it's important to know a bit about theater traditions, superstitions, and folklore.

**Never say "Macbeth" in a theater.** It's traditional to avoid uttering the word "Macbeth" inside a theater. Actors, stagehands, and theater patrons refer to the play as "that Scottish play," and they call its leading-lady character "Lady M." If one does say "Macbeth" inside a theater, he must promptly exit the theater, spin three times counterclockwise, spit, swear, and then knock on the theater door and ask to be let back in. If that "undoing" ritual is not conducted, the curse of Macbeth will bring bad luck, leading to accidents on set and catastrophes in the lives of the performers and staff. Granted, *Macbeth* has more swordfights than most other plays, which in itself increases the chances of accidents. However, there are many stories of theater personnel thinking the superstition was silly and subsequently suffering the consequences with minor accidents and bad luck.

There are various theories about the Macbeth curse. Some say that the lines Shakespeare wrote for the three witches are actual incantations, and that therefore each performance of the play casts forth spells and curses. Others believe *Macbeth* is cursed because, being a crowd-pleasing production, theater owners would stage it as a last-ditch effort to save a struggling theater. Sadly, within weeks of the play's performance, the troubled theater would be out of business anyway; thus *The Tragedy of Macbeth* became a "kiss of death" production.

**Don't say "good luck"; say "break a leg."** This superstition started because actors believed "theater sprites" would ramp up their mischievous behavior upon hearing the words "good luck." In an effort to throw the sprites off track, the actors instead wished each other something that sounded horrible and painful, such as "Break a leg." On the positive side, it means the actor has to get down on bended knee to accept thunderous applause.

**Don't whistle in a theater.** In the early theater days, many stagehands were former sailors. Sailors often communicated with each other using various whistles. Theater people employed this same method of communication to cue the raising or lowering of scenery, props, and curtains. Whistling for any other reason was discouraged in theaters because such whistles could be mistaken as a cue, causing a backdrop to be lowered at the wrong time. Today, actors believe that whistling in their dressing room or at any time during rehearsal will doom the production.

**Avoid green costumes.** The color green is traditionally avoided in costumes because before electric stage lighting, lime was burned to illumiunate the stage, and its greenish glow overpowered any green colors on stage. This is where the expression "in the limelight" comes from. In early plays, yellow and green symbolized the devil, so these colors are considered taboo in costumes.

**Beware of peacocks and cats.** It's considered bad luck to have a peacock or its feathers on stage; the eye of the bird's feather is believed to be the Evil Eye, which will curse the play. Cats can be good-luck charms for theaters as long as they remain in the wings or backstage. A black cat rubbing the leg of a performer supposedly blesses the actor with an exceptional performance. However, a black cat crossing the stage is considered an evil portent.

**The final line of the play is not spoken during rehearsal.** Thespians reserve the last line of the play for the live performance. When the last line is spoken during a performance, the play is finished, but if it's spoken outside of a performance, the play is *finished!* Theater people also believe that a perfect rehearsal means the play will fail and close quickly.

**No Bibles on stage—and no knitting.** Bibles are not to be used as props; to do so would be disrespectful and therefore bad luck. If a play requires a bible on stage, a regular book is painted to look like a bible. Knitting is also prohibited from the stage; it's believed that knitting will lock in the mistakes during the rehearsal by weaving them permanently into the production. Of course, pointed objects such as knitting needles have inherent danger.

**Show you care by being careful with flowers.** There are many superstitions about flowers in the theater. Never send flowers to the actress before the show, as it will bring bad luck. Yellow flowers are a no-no because, as previously mentioned, yellow and green originally represented the devil on stage. It's proper to give flowers to the lead actress before the final curtain on opening night, and she must keep them in her dressing room for the duration of the play's run no matter how wilted they become. Disposing of them sooner ensures the early cancellation of the production. Also, real flowers are never used as props on stage; since they require water, there is a risk that the water will spill and cause an actor to slip.

**If you must open an umbrella in a theater, do it with the point down.** In general, it's considered bad luck to open an umbrella indoors. This belief originated in a theater in 1868. An orchestra leader named Bob Williams opened his umbrella inside a theater before stepping out into the rain on his way to a weekend boat trip. As the boat pulled away from the dock, one of the engines blew, killing Williams instantly. Sometimes an actor must open an umbrella indoors as part of the show; as a protective measure, he will point the umbrella toward the ground while opening it.

**The theater must never be dark.** The belief is that ghosts will take over a darkened theater, so theaters often have what's called a "ghost light" which is always on whenever a performance is not in progress. Carnegie Hall uses a ghost light. According to Gino Francesconi, the director of Carnegie Hall's archives and museum, "a 'ghost light' or 'ghost lamp' prevents the theater from being haunted. It is a bare bulb left on stage on nights when the theater is dark. Basically, it's to fool the ghosts into thinking a performance is taking place so that they don't take over with one of their own! It is an old superstition practiced by many theaters around the world and something the public rarely sees. I have heard many explanations of how it came to pass, one being that a burglar or producer of a show was walking back into a dark theater after opening night and fell into the pit and was killed. He threatened to haunt the place forever if a light wasn't left on to prevent others from falling into the pit."

As evidence of the success of Carnegie Hall's ghost light, Francesconi said, "People have been born and died here and I've never heard about one ghost story in thirty-six years." However, legendary romantic singer Johnny Mathis claimed he witnessed a ghost at Carnegie Hall while rehearsing for his October 1993 concert. Mathis even mentioned this during a television interview on *Good Morning America*, but the host quickly changed the subject.

# CHAPTER 25

# Cherry Lane Theater

THIS INTIMATE THEATER, located at 38 Commerce Street, was the brainchild of Edna St. Vincent Millay in 1924. She formed an experimental theater group of local artists in the former brewery and box factory building, which dates back to

1836. Although there have never been any cherry trees along Commerce Street, the theater's name fosters that notion. The reality is that Millay had named her group "The Cheery Lane Theater" to play on "Dreary Lane," the nickname of the Drury Lane Theater in London. But a reporter misstated the name as "Cherry Lane," and that's what stuck.

Over the years there have been reports of ghosts "performing" at the theater. Sightings include a white mist that forms on the top step of the lobby staircase and a shadowy manifestation that hovers around the hallway outside the dressing rooms. Three former residents of the neighborhood—Aaron Burr, Washington Irving, and Thomas Paine—have been suspected as the identity of these phantoms.

Of course, a possible recent addition to the ghostly cast may be the spirit of Kim Hunter, the Oscar-winning actress best known for playing Stella in the stage and screen versions of Tennessee Williams' *A Streetcar Named Desire*. In 1954, Hunter moved into an apartment above the Cherry Lane Theater with her husband, Robert Emmett. Kim's career was derailed for a short time in the 1950s when she was blacklisted by McCarthy as a communist sympathizer. Hunter was no such thing. She was, however, according to her obituary in the *New York Times*, "feisty" and "occasionally profane," with "no use for the trappings of Hollywood stardom that had always eluded her." Hunter was quoted as saying: "The work itself has been my life. I was never in this for jazzy stardom, and as far as that's concerned, I've never had it. Doesn't matter to me." Hunter's husband died in 2000, and Kim Hunter died September 12, 2002. Maybe she was just too feisty for a final bow and stays active near the other love of her life, the stage at the Cherry Lane.

I spoke with Alex, the theater manager at the Cherry Lane, who has worked there for three and a half years. He said he has not experienced anything paranormal there, even though he has been in the theater very late at night. He did say, though: "We like to think that the spirit of Edna [Millay] keeps an eye on the place. I always say, 'Good morning, Edna,' or 'Good night, Edna,' when coming or going."

Why not visit the Cherry Lane Theater? You can make a ghostly night out of it and have dinner and a show; the One If By Land, Two If By Sea restaurant (the subject of an earlier chapter in this book) is within walking distance.

# CHAPTER 26

# New Amsterdam Theater

THE BEAUTIFUL ART-NOUVEAU New Amsterdam Theater dates back to 1903, the days of stage grandeur. Located in Times Square, this theater was the home of Ziegfeld's *Follies* from 1913 to 1927, when programs such as "Midnight Frolic" and "The Nine O'clock Revue" were performed on the rooftop stage.

In order to appreciate the famous ghost of the New Amsterdam theater, you must know a bit about who she was when she was alive. She was born Oliveretta Duffy and lived in Pittsburgh, Pennsylvania. At the age of sixteen, she married Bernard Krug Thomas. The unhappy marriage was terminated by divorce two years later, in 1915, and Olive Thomas went to live with relatives in Harlem. She worked the counter in the basement of a department store, but she managed to change her life by calling in sick one day. Instead of reporting to work, she stood in line to be judged for a contest called "The Most Beautiful Girl in New York City," organized by commercial artist Howard Chandler Christy. Olive Thomas's Irish beauty—her dark hair, blue-violet eyes, long dark lashes, rosebud lips, and porcelain skin—won her the title, and her picture appeared in the newspaper.

Florenz Ziegfeld saw the picture in the paper and just had to have this beauty in his *Follies*. Olive accepted the offer. Eventually, Ziegfeld promoted Olive to his more risqué program, *Frolics*. In this production, the girls were clad in balloons, and the wealthy gents who came to drink and watch the show would delight in popping the balloons with their lit cigars. For a time, Ziegfeld and Olive had an affair, but Ziegfeld soon moved on to the next "new girl." Olive, though, was smart enough to stay friendly with Ziegfeld; she didn't burn any bridges.

By 1916, Olive moved west in search of a career in motion pictures. In Hollywood, she met Jack Pickford, younger brother of Mary Pickford. Jack was an actor, not at his sister's level of fame, but recognized nonetheless. Olive and Jack fell head over heels in love, and they married in 1917. Jack's family did not accept Olive, given her prior work in the *Frolics* and her having received admiration and expensive gifts from so many men. It was said that the German Ambassador Bernstorff gave Olive a pearl necklace worth $10,000. However, that family tension wasn't the reason that Olive kept her marriage to Jack a secret for the first year. She wanted to make it on her own in Hollywood; she didn't want people to say she had glided in on the wings of the Pickford name.

Olive's and Jack's marriage was stormy, due not only to the long separations inherent in the movie industry but also to Jack's drinking, gambling, and drug abuse. Olive's career, on the other hand, was highly successful; she appeared in a total of twenty-three silent movies.

By June of 1920, the couple had separated, but in August they reunited and decided to take a second honeymoon in Paris to celebrate. The Pickfords met friends and enjoyed an evening of partying and dining in the Monmartre section of Paris. They returned to their hotel suite at 3:30 A.M., and Jack suggested they pack in the morning for their departure to London. He went straight to sleep. Olive was unable to sleep and went into the bathroom to take some sleeping medication. Leaving the light off for fear of waking her husband, she took a bottle from the medicine chest and drank from it. Almost immediately she collapsed to the floor, exclaiming, "Oh, my God! I'm poisoned!" Jack rushed into the bathroom, turned on the light, and found her on the floor. He took her in his arms and found the cobalt bottle. Even though the label was in French, he knew she was poisoned: The bottle contained mercurial bichloride, his medication for the treatment of syphilis, and it was only to be applied topically.

Jack called the doctor; while waiting for him to arrive, Jack had Olive drink water in the hopes of inducing vomiting. He said, "I forced the whites of eggs down her throat, hoping to offset the poison. The doctor came. He pumped her stomach three times while I held

Olive."

Olive was taken to the Neuilly Hospital, where for five days she clung to life. All hope of recovery was lost, though, once her kidneys became paralyzed; within hours, she was dead. She was only twenty-six years old.

The French medical examiner determined the cause of death to be accidental poisoning. Rumors circulated that Jack had intentionally poisoned her, but he was never formally charged. Other rumors claimed that Olive was so depressed, she killed herself. The suicide theory may have some merit; according to the doctor, even if she had taken the sleeping medicine, the amount she drank still would have been lethal.

Arrangements were made to send Olive's body back to New York City for a funeral at the Church of the Holy Trinity. Aboard the ship, the distraught Jack attempted to kill himself by jumping overboard. Fortunately, he was restrained by other passengers. Ziegfeld paid for the pricey funeral, which was attended by four thousand mourners, and for the burial at the elegant Woodlawn cemetery in the Bronx. Olive was buried in a white gown with a gold sash draped over one shoulder.

No sooner was Olive Thomas Pickford interred than reports started to surface that stage hands had seen Olive backstage at the New Amsterdam Theater in her *Follies* green-beaded costume and matching hat. Rumors flew of people seeing shadows in the wings and losing objects that reappeared in strange places backstage.

The incident that confirmed the identity of the spirit was the sighting, several years later, of a full-body apparition of the gorgeous Olive Thomas Pickford. An electrician told some stagehands that he had seen the most beautiful girl on stage when he came in early that morning. One of the stagehands revealed that he had seen the same young beauty years earlier. He remembered the same white dress and gold sash. Later, the electrician and the stagehand went through some pictures and memorabilia and identified one of the girls in *Follies* cast pictures as the ghost they had seen. It was Olive.

The New Amsterdam became a movie house in 1937; it went downhill from there. By 1981, it had closed. Happily, it reopened in April 1997, its art-nouveau stage fully restored to its former beauty by the new lessee, the Disney Corporation. Dana Amendola was the manager in charge of the theater then. He had hired a security guard to patrol the theater overnight. The guard called Amendola at 2:30 in the morning in a state of panic. He said he had been walking across the stage, using his flashlight to inspect the area, when suddenly his light illuminated a vision of a young woman in a green beaded dress and headpiece holding a little blue bottle. The security guard thereafter refused to work at the New Amsterdam.

Amendola researched the history of the theater and, of course, came across the story of Olive Thomas Pickford. He questioned the workers who had done the restoration work prior to the 1997 reopening. They confirmed they had seen the beauty with the blue vial on several occasions. They reported further that sometimes the ghostly young woman would speak in a light, happy, flirty voice, saying, "Hi, fella!"

To this day, two portraits of Olive hang backstage, and it is theater policy that employees say, "Good morning, Olive!" when they arrive at work and "Good night, Olive!" when they leave. This seems to keep the gentle but somewhat temperamental spirit appeased. Olive is troublesome whenever major changes are made in her theater, as well as when her contemporaries return to visit it. It's reported that when the Broadway Cares/Equity Fights AIDS invited surviving *Follies* cast members to attend an "Easter Bonnet" competition, the sets began to shake violently. During another "Bonnet" competition for former *Follies* members, all the light bulbs burned out on one of the office floors. No electrical malfunction was found.

I've been to the New Amsterdam Theater several times over the years to see various productions. This was the first time I had visited to inspect it from the paranormal point of view. Unfortunately, asking for help at the theater box office yielded only a telephone number that no one ever answers. And forget getting a call returned; I think I have a better shot at capturing a full-body apparition. I hung around the lobby a while, covertly recording with my digital audio device, but it captured no sounds other than the banging of doors and occasional street noise as people walked in and out. But I had that feeling—you know, the one that says, "If I had known then what I know now!"

As I'm writing this, *Mary Poppins* is playing at the New Amsterdam. Looks like I will have to buy a ticket to get in and find Olive. Oh, and since Olive makes herself visible after the theater has emptied, I will have to hang in the ladies' room for a little while. Maybe I'll see you there—or, better still, maybe you'll see Olive.

In case you aren't aware of it, there is a daily lottery for discounted tickets to various Broadway shows. Well ahead of curtain time or by the posted lottery time, you arrive at the theater of the show you want to see, and you write your name and the number of tickets you want (usually two is the limit) on a slip of paper. The slips are collected in a drum. At a set time, an employee draws slips from the drum, and those whose names are called can purchase discount tickets to the show. Everybody who enters has the same chance of winning, and there's no need to line up in the middle of the night. A good strategy is to take a friend with you so that he or she can enter too. Hopefully, one of you will be called. To further increase your chances of success, choose an evening performance on a Tuesday, Wednesday, or Thursday.

# CHAPTER 27

# Palace Theater

LONG BEFORE WE HAD *Star Search* or *American Idol*, there was "the beach" on the sidewalk in front of the Palace Theater. Performers came from all around to show off their talents here, hoping for an invitation from one of the Palace managers to perform on stage. Martin Beck, who opened the Palace in 1913, touted the theater as "the Valhalla of Vaudeville." Playing at the

Palace meant a performer had "made it." Celebrity greats such as Jack Benny, Sarah Bernhardt, Irving Berlin, Fanny Brice, and Judy Garland all performed there.

During the Great Depression in the 1930s, the Palace suffered and was forced to convert to the more lucrative business of being a movie house. In the 1950s, the Palace attempted to recapture its vaudeville glory days by bringing in acts such as jugglers and tumblers. This is how the most famous ghost legend at the Palace was born. An acrobatic high-wire act called The Four Casting Pearls was known for performing without a safety net; tragically, during a show at the Palace, Louis Borsalino fell from the tightrope, broke his neck, and died. People have reported hearing his screams and fall; unnerving as that would be, it is said to be a good omen. Conversely, *seeing* Louis fall to his death is said to portend imminent death for the witness.

Judy Garland had her own stage door constructed at the rear of the Palace orchestra. In October 1995, psychic medium Elizabeth Baron conducted psychic readings at the Palace at the request of much of the cast and crew of *Beauty and the Beast*. Baron claimed to channel the spirit of Judy Garland, who had messages for her daughter Liza Minnelli. Baron also claimed that there are over one hundred other spirits of performers residing at the Palace Theater, still waiting for their big break.

It's possible that hundreds of ghosts are waiting for their big break, as Baron suggested. I suspect, though, that there may be some residual energy from a fire at the theater on February 17, 1932. A lamp short-circuited and fell over, igniting the curtains, which sent flames dashing out into the audience. In the stampede that ensued, seven of the 1,900 people in the theater were injured, including a few who were severely burned. The majority of the people were at least bruised from the stampede.

Actress Andrea McArdle, while performing in *Beauty and the Beast* in 1995, saw the ghost of a white-gowned cellist playing in the orchestra pit. Other ghosts that have been reported at the Palace include a little girl who looks down from the balcony with a sad expression on her face, and the ghost of a little boy who plays with his toy trucks on the landing behind the mezzanine. Office workers have seen the ghost of a man in a brown suit strutting briskly past their office doors; when they check to see who it was, they find no one there.

I couldn't find a physical description of the forlorn little girl in the balcony, but I think she might be associated with the 1914 arrest of an actress named Mary Cameron. Mary was an actress who put her skills to work cashing bogus checks at several hotels in Manhattan. On June 13, 1914, she appeared at the front desk of the Manhattan Hotel with a ten-year-old girl and registered as Mrs. V. Maxwell. She made a show of pretending to be a long-time patron of the hotel. She went on to tell the clerk that she had her trunks at a friend's place at West 72nd Street, and she requested that a porter go retrieve them for her. Continuing her performance, she told the clerk with feigned embarrassment that she had left her purse in one of the trunks, and she asked the clerk to please cash a $40 check to tide her over until her trunks arrived. Clerks at the Manhattan, Algonquin, and Belleclaire hotels fell for her act, cashing checks ranging from $25 to $50. Once she had the cash, she would say she was off to the drug store to pick up a few items, never to return. Only when the porters returned, reporting that the address Cameron gave was a vacant lot, did the hotel clerks realize they had been scammed.

The curtain came down on Mary Cameron's act on Sunday, August 9, 1914. When she attempted to cash a $25 check at the Hotel University, the clerk realized Cameron fit the description of the woman wanted by the police, so he hesitated. Cameron quickly exited the hotel, but four detectives followed her to the Palace Theater, where they cornered her on the sixth-floor fire escape. During her arrest, Cameron became hysterical and began to faint but was revived with water. She continued her hysteria through the arraignment and refused to plead to the charge of passing a worthless $40 check to the Manhattan Hotel.

So the question remains: Who was the ten-year-old girl with Mary Cameron at the Manhattan Hotel? Did the child witness Cameron's dramatic arrest at the Palace Theater, and is that why her little spirit is trapped there? Perhaps another ghosthunter attending a show at the Palace will find the answers to those questions.

I spoke with Dixon Rosario, theater manager at the Palace and an employee of the Nederland Company for the past thirty years. Dixon heard the theater was haunted when he started with the company, but he didn't believe it. He told me that back in the 1990s, *Will Rogers' Follies* was playing at the Palace. During intermission, Dixon went to check on things in the lobby. A woman came up to him and asked him if it was customary for the performers to come out to the lobby at intermission. He told her it wasn't, but she insisted that she had seen a ballerina in a pink tutu walk through the lobby. Dixon insisted that the show was a Western and no ballet dancers were in the production. Dixon thought the encounter was strange, but he dismissed it and went about his business. Later, Dixon would think back on this rather odd conversation and realize the woman had seen a ghost.

In January of 2007, Dixon had his own eye-opening experience with the mischievous ghosts of the Palace Theater. The theater was dark, awaiting the arrival of *Legally Blonde*. Therefore, Dixon was filling in as manager over at the Richard Rogers Theater. He went to his office at the Palace to change into a suit before heading to the Richard Rogers. Dixon laid his belt on the chair by his desk, then went to the bathroom to brush his teeth. He came back into his office and proceeded to get dressed. When he reached for his belt, it wasn't on the chair. He figured it may have slipped to the floor, so he pulled out the chair and looked.

It wasn't there. He checked all over, under, and around his desk and chair. No belt. Soon, he was retracing his steps and checking the sofa, the closet, the hallway; still, he couldn't find the belt. Rather than be late to work at the Richard Rogers Theater, he left without the belt, hoping his pants would stay up. After he was finished at the Richard Rogers Theater, he came back to his office at the Palace. As soon as he turned his office light on, he saw his belt lying across the chair at the desk, right where he had originally placed it. This was Dixon's chilling "a ha" moment.

These days, Dixon is accustomed to some of the paranormal events. When he sees a figure walk past his office door, he no longer wastes his breath calling out, "Who's there?" He knows he's alone, at least in the physical sense. He's grown accustomed to things on his desk being moved or hidden under papers. To avoid an aggravating search for his keys, he's gotten in the habit of leaving them in the lock of the office door.

In early 2010, Dixon had one other experience of the paranormal kind. It was close to 7:30 P.M., and he was about to open the theater doors to let the audience in. He was conferring with the ticket taker while standing on the left side of the third lobby. Dixon told me: "We were standing about three feet apart and talking. This *distortion* moved right between us. I don't know how to explain it other than it was like I could see through it, but it was distorted." I asked him if it had an appearance like the heat waves coming up off the road in the summertime. He said, "You know, I never thought of it like that. That's a perfect way to describe it." He went on to say that the ticket taker looked at him and said, "Did you see that?" and Dixon confirmed that he had.

Another possible ghost at the Palace may be that of a stage-hand who fell from the catwalks and died in the 1980s. He was only twenty-six years old. Perhaps this young man's spirit is trapped in the theater because either he doesn't know he's dead or he feels guilty that he wasn't more careful.

On April 5, 2010, I was able to meet with Mr. Richard Melina, a porter who has worked at the Palace Theater for nineteen years. He was kind enough to let my son, my mother, and me into the theater while it was dark. Melina sat with us and told us of his paranormal experiences while working at the theater. He said: "Years ago, a psychic with very good credentials was compelled to come to the theater. She insisted that all the theater personnel gather on the stage. While on her way to the stage, she waited in one corner of the hallway. I could tell she was in excruciating pain. Finally, she broke free from the pain and was able to tell me that the name of the ghost who wanted her attention in that moment was Jaco." Melina recognized the name as that of a musician at a club where he worked as a bouncer in the 1980s. Jaco Pastorius, the famous jazz bassist, was out of control one night at the club where Melina worked, and Melina was tasked with subduing Jaco to get him into an ambulance so he could be taken to the hospital. Melina remembers that the last thing he saw Jaco do was "flip me both birds as they closed the ambulance doors." The psychic went on to say that Jaco later died at the hands of a bouncer at a club in Florida. Just as the psychic was saying how Jaco died, a theater employee walked past Melina carrying a book written by Jaco. Melina told me, "It felt like Jaco was giving me the finger from the grave."

Melina said the only voice he has ever heard in the theater was in the back of the house. While behind the sound board and control panel, he heard a man's voice say the word "Canada" twice. When he turned to see who said it, there was no one there.

Melina has also heard the jingling of dog tags and leashes near the Coke machine by the lockers; this is where "the Mad Capped Mutts," the dogs in the *Will Rogers' Follies* show, were kept in preparation for their stage entrance. Eddie, another theater employee, joined the conversation and confirmed that he has heard the dogs barking. Sadly, those dogs died right outside the palace, locked in a van that burned when a nightlight caught the dashboard on fire. Melina said he had been very fond of the dogs, and that he took care of them when their owners vacationed in Florida. Every so often, he says, the dogs let him know they're still there by giving him a little push in the small of his back, just as they used to do when they were ready to go on stage.

Melina then led us to the stage, past the Coke machine and an elevator that was installed for Sarah Bernhardt. He explained that Bernhardt had a wooden leg and needed the elevator to get to the stage. Also, he told us, Bernhardt didn't trust U.S. currency and demanded to be paid in gold, so a safe was installed to store the gold, which was paid to her before each performance.

The minute we arrived on stage, I took a picture of the ghost light (ghost lights are explained on page 165). An orb appeared in that first picture but in none of the other pictures I subsequently took of the ghost light. I did find orbs in some of the pictures I took from the mezzanines. Most of them were dust-borne, but a couple appeared to have a genuine spirit energy in that they emitted their own light and appeared in one picture but not the next.

On the upper mezzanine, my son Brian got a slight chill while filming with the camcorder. We found nothing in our photos, audio recordings, or temperature readings to suggest the chill had been paranormal in origin. Shortly after Brian experienced the chill, I had a "head rush" as I walked through the same area. I turned around quickly after that sensation and took a picture, which revealed two faint orbs near the carpet. Could they represent the ghost boy and girl, or were they more likely caused by dust my feet had stirred up?

Next, we walked down the stairs to the lower mezzanine, and Melina pointed out the beautiful marble that had been restored by removing the yellow paint that had covered it. We stopped at the display case with the theater memorabilia, then went to what had formerly been Judy Garland's stage door. Mr. Melina explained that the door has been repositioned slightly since Judy used it, due to a modification made to the stairs above it. I kept my audio recorder on this entire time, but it captured no EVPs.

Our last stop was the orchestra section of the house. Brian and I went down to the orchestra pit area to record for EVPs and possibly to take a picture of the ghost cellist. Unfortunately, the house lights could not be shut off completely because two men were painting in the upper box seats section. Our audio and video recordings near the orchestra pit captured nothing paranormal. As we were exiting the house, Melina pointed out the control booth where he had been standing the time he heard a male voice behind him say "Canada" twice.

In my own way, I "played the Palace." I was on the same stage used by Judy Garland, and I stood where Louis Borsalino died after falling from the high wire. Although the theater looked empty, it didn't *feel* empty. I made my exit, stage left—but for the ghosts of the Palace Theater, the show must go on, and on.

# Spotlight: Times Square

The most famous spot in New York City has to be Times Square. It's appeared in countless movies, such as *Big, I Am Legend,* and *Jerry McGuire.* Certainly everyone recognizes it as the place to watch the ball drop on New Year's Eve. In fact, Web cams make it possible to view this legendary location from anywhere in the world all year long.

Times Square draws people from all over the globe, in this life and the afterlife. Case in point: two Royal Air Force pilots who appeared mysteriously on the corner of 45th Street in Times Square during World War II. They asked Harvard graduate Oswald Reinsen, who was standing next to them on the corner, whether they were in Times Square. He confirmed their location, then began to cross the street. They followed him. Noticing the pilots' uniforms and their English accents, Reinsen struck up a conversation with them. They told him how determined they were to visit Times Square. Reinsen

noticed they kept a close eye on the time, checking their watches habitually every ten minutes or so. After walking several blocks, Reinsen reached his destination, the Harvard Club. He invited the RAF men to join him, and they gladly accepted.

They enjoyed dinner and "spirited" conversation; all the while, the two RAF men kept checking the time on their watches. Just before midnight, they explained that it had been close to twenty-four hours since their planes had been shot down over Berlin. As they rose from their seats, they thanked Reinsen for the meal and proceeded toward the exit. Reinsen watched, dumbfounded, as they got lost in the crowd and vanished from view.

That story may be the most extensive and intense example ever of a crisis apparition. A typical crisis apparition occurs immediately after death. The newly deceased, without the trappings of his corporeal being, "makes the rounds" by showing up to loved ones as a final farewell. Here's how a crisis apparition works: You answer the doorbell, and there's your Uncle Ted. You're excited to see him

and invite him in. Knowing how sick he's been with cancer, you can't believe how great he looks and that he is out and about. You make him comfortable on the couch and dash off to the kitchen to make him a cup of tea. All the while you're chatting at a thousand words a minute and not realizing Uncle Ted isn't responding. You come back to the living room with his cup of tea, and he is gone. As you call out for him, the telephone rings. You answer the phone, and your Aunt Bette says that Uncle Ted just died.

Most crisis apparitions appear as solid as you and I. Some may speak, but that's rare. As an example of how solid they can appear, I know of a woman who bumped into the crisis apparition of her father. She worked in New York City, and her demanding job had her rushing from one meeting to the next. While she was racing to pick up a sandwich and head to the next meeting, she was checking messages on her cell phone. Someone bumped into her, and when she looked up from her phone long enough to give the person a nasty look, she saw her father. He waved to her and vanished in the crowd. She wondered why her father was in New York City, but she continued to rush to her meeting, figuring she'd see him back at her office later. She had enough time to inhale her sandwich, shut off her cell phone, and sit down for the start of the meeting.

After the meeting, she checked her messages and heard a heartbreaking one from her mother that said, "Daddy had a heart attack. He's dead. I need you to come home right away." Once home, she learned that her father had died around the time she bumped into him on the street. He had come to New York to wave a final good-bye.

# CHAPTER 28

# Paradise Theater

LOEW'S PARADISE THEATER, a gem on the Grand Concourse in the Bronx, opened on September 7, 1929. Its designer,
John Eberson, spent $4,000,000 recreating the atmosphere of
an Italian garden with beautiful cherub statuary, gilded pillars
and light fixtures, and a twinkling nighttime sky projected onto
the ceiling above the stage. This theater in the Bronx is one of
the few and best remaining examples of Eberson's creative work,
as his Paradise Theater in Chicago was demolished in 1956.

A concrete slab was fitted over the orchestra pit in the 1940s
to accommodate four additional rows of seats. This slab was
lifted once, in the 1960s, to remove the pipe organ, which was
installed at the Loew's in Jersey City, New Jersey. The multiplex-
theater fad arrived at the Paradise starting in 1973, when it was

converted in to a duplex; in 1975, it became a triplex. By 1981, the theater had been modified yet again to house four screens, but it could no longer sustain the multiplex business model, and it closed in 1994.

The Paradise sat unused until Richard DeCesare, a contractor from Westchester, signed a ten-year lease for the property in April 1999. He hired an architectural and engineering firm to restore the theater, along with historic preservation consultants to oversee the historical accuracy of the renovation and to work with the city's Landmarks Preservation Commission. Unfortunately, DeCesare had bit off far more than he could chew, financially speaking. From 2000 to 2003, renovations ceased and the theater was locked up. When new owners took over in 2003, they completed the renovation and maintained the building's integrity as a stage performance theater with a re-opening in 2005. Joe Gentile took over as manager of the theater in 2007, but within months, the theater closed again. The current managers, Messrs. Sanders, Joyner, and Boter, took control in September 2009 and reopened the theater on October 24, 2009, with a concert by Charlie Wilson of The Gap Band.

I investigated the Paradise Theater in 2003, when its future was still uncertain. Thankfully, the Paradise today is open for business, which means I can include it in this book for your ghosthunting exploration. Let's rewind to Halloween 2003, when I conducted my investigation.

On October 30, 2003, I was just pulling into the driveway as my cell phone rang. I answered the call hesitantly, as I didn't recognize the phone number. It was a woman from Telemundo, the largest Latin-American television network, asking me if I had ever been to the Paradise Theater in the Bronx. I told her I hadn't ever been there, and she proceeded to ask me if I would be available to go there the following day—Halloween—to investigate it with one of their field correspondents and a cameraman.

**The beautiful interior of the Paradise Theater**

Luckily, the time that they wanted to shoot this news clip was in between two other presentations that I was scheduled to make that evening.

The next day, I did my morning presentation, then made a quick dash to Target to buy a lightweight top, as it was an unseasonably warm day. With my "ghost gear" in the car, I drove to Teterboro, New Jersey, to meet Sam Rivera at the Telemundo office. Sam explained to me that he went to the Paradise Theater once before to follow up on a story. As they filmed his closing statement for that news piece, an amorphous, moving shadow appeared in the lower left corner of the shot. The shadow was not discovered until the cameraman was reviewing the footage back at the studio. Sam hunted desperately through the footage, trying to explain the shadow, but he could not find its source. The cameraman had been in the upper rows of the balcony, aiming his camera down, as Sam sat on the railing of the balcony. Therefore, no curtains or loose tarps had been in proximity to cast such a shadow. Sam showed me the footage, and I could see that he was perfectly illuminated and centered in the frame. This shadow simply wasn't possible given the lighting at the time. Needless to say, I was excited to get to this theater and check it out.

Sam, the cameraman, and I left Teterboro in the news van loaded with cameras and microphones, crossed the George Washington Bridge, and headed up to the Bronx. We arrived at the theater by 1 P.M. and were greeted by security guard Fred Martinez. Fred warned us that the lights in the theater were not yet wired, so we prepared our equipment, microphones, and cameras in the outer lobby using the available daylight. Construction materials such as cans of paint, piles of drywall, and sawhorses were strewn about. The statuary was covered in plastic to protect it during the renovations. The whole renovation project looked like a grand-scale version of my second husband's affliction, S.B.D.F. (Started But Didn't Finish). Remember, at this time, DeCesare's renovations had stopped because he ran out of money, and the new owners had just acquired the property.

We entered the Paradise Theater on the main level via the grand lobby. The four thousand seats that used to occupy this space had been removed for the renovations, making the 45,000-square-foot space feel even larger. We had to navigate through the darkness using only the light from our cameras and flashlights. Fred Martinez led us down the side of the theater toward the stage. We climbed the stage, and Martinez told us about a noise he heard periodically from the stage area. He described it as the sound of two metal doors banging together. Every time he investigated the sound, he couldn't determine what was causing it. The backstage doors to the alley were secure. Martinez even tested for the sound by unlocking the backstage doors and slamming and banging on them, but their sounds were not the same as the banging sound he'd heard. Fred asked us to remain quiet for a few minutes to listen for the mysterious noise. Suddenly, we heard it. The cameraman caught it on film as well. I asked Fred to take us to the alley; I wanted to see if there was room for a car to drive through and possibly rattle a loose sewer cover. The alley was far too narrow for a vehicle to pass through, and there were no metal covers to rattle. Nor were there any of those metal chutes that are often used to dispose of construction debris from upper floors of buildings.

We returned to the main theater level, where I took some pictures. I should clarify that I was using a Sony Mavica digital camera, a 1.0 megapixel camera that was, at that time, top of the line. Today's cell phones take pictures at 3 megapixels! Since those days, paranormal investigators have learned a lot about orbs. It seems that if you set your digital camera to take the largest image it can (that is, its highest megapixel setting), you eliminate a lot of dust orbs that are caused by airborne particulates. Needless to say, using a 1-megapixel camera in a theater full of construction dust, I was capturing a lot of orbs. I followed protocol, though; each time I took a picture that resulted in orbs, I stayed in the same spot and took several more pictures to compare and contrast the results. Dust travels in herds and will be in photo after photo; whereas a genuine spirit energy orb will emit its own light and be in one photo and not the next as they move so rapidly.

We walked down the long hallway to access the stairs to the balcony. What little I could see in the dim light of my flashlight was ornate Baroque moldings on the walls and ceiling. I could tell that this theater had been breathtaking in its heyday. We climbed the stairs to the balcony, and Sam showed me where he had been standing when the shadow was filmed. He then turned and told me a story that he believes explains the identity of the shadow or "phantasmos." About a year before the filming of the shadow, a young man running from police had ducked into the theater, and the police, along with his wife and children, followed. His wife was begging him to turn himself in. He ran up to the balcony, thinking he could get to a roof portal. However, when he reached the last row of the balcony, he realized there was no way out. The police, his wife, and his children were on the lower landing of the balcony. Frustrated and determined not go to jail, he told his family he loved them, then turned his gun and shot himself in the head.

Sam said that the day the shadow was seen on film, the cameraman had been in the last row of the balcony, the area where the young man committed suicide. Sam was positioned where the police and family members had been. In fact, that was the story Sam had been sent to the theater to follow up on. When he found the shadow on the film, Sam figured a follow-up report would be a perfect Halloween news piece, and therefore he arranged for Telemundo to return to the Paradise with me in tow. I took a couple of pictures of the balcony, then climbed toward the last row. When I was about twenty feet from the back of the balcony, I got a picture of an orb. I stood still and continued to take several more pictures. No other orbs appeared. No one else had been up here, and I hadn't reached the last row to stir up dust in the area where the orb appeared. I had the unnerving feeling that this orb indicated the presence of the suicide victim. I showed the picture to Sam, and he included it in the news piece. The cameraman told me that the day he filmed the shadow, he felt anxious at the top of the balcony, but he attributed it to his fear of heights. However, when he saw the film footage with the moving shadow, he understood that the emotional remnant of a ghost had caused his anxiety.

I searched the archives of the *New York Times* for articles about this man's suicide, and I had the reference librarian of the

New York Public Library search for articles, but nothing turned up to substantiate Sam's story. Therefore, I am telling it as I remember him telling it to me.

We stayed in the balcony for a while, taking thermal scan readings and more photos. I also recorded for EVPs on my digital audio recorder. While the audio recorder didn't catch any EVPs in the balcony area, it did pick up the earlier banging noises from backstage.

Sam said then that we had to get back to the studio in order to get the piece edited and ready for the six o'clock news, so we went back to the outer lobby to pack up our gear. We got back to the studio in record time and filmed the evidence-review segment in the studio. Sam kindly gave me a VHS copy of the segment, and I was on my way in time to make my evening presentation.

I went back to the Paradise Theater in February of 2010 to take pictures for this book. I spoke with the lady in the box office about the man who had supposedly shot himself in the theater. She said she remembered hearing something about that but didn't know the entire story. She was unable to let me in to take pictures of the theater as the managers weren't available to give approval, but she let me take a picture of the outer lobby. Fortunately, pictures of the renovated theater can be seen at the official website, http://www.paradisetheaterevents.com.

If I get a chance to see a show at the Paradise Theater, I'm requesting a seat in the back row of the balcony. It's probably the cheapest seat in the house, and yet, for a ghosthunter, it's the best.

# CHAPTER 29

# Public Theater

TODAY, THE PUBLIC THEATER is a multiplex-style stage theater that provides entertainment via various productions on several stages. Originally, this building was the Astor Library, built by John Jacob Astor in 1853. Located in the East Village on Lafayette Street, the Public Theater is within walking distance of the Merchant's House (page 113) and St. Mark's Church in-the-Bowery (page 52).

Dr. Joseph Green Cogswell, who in 1820 was a professor of mineralogy and geology at Harvard University, was one of the founders of the Astor Library project. Cogswell was appointed the superintendent of the library in 1848. Working late one night in 1859, he heard a noise and went to investigate it, knowing he was the only one in the building at the time. He went past a few

Kenneth Leslie has worked as a security guard at the theater for over ten years.

rows of stacks and turned a corner to find a frail, elderly man hunched over his books, reading and writing notes in the dimly lit area. Cogswell recognized the man as Washington Irving, but realized it couldn't possibly be him. Irving, one of the original founders of the Astor Library, had died several months before. In fact, the last time Cogswell saw Irving was at his funeral.

A few evenings later, Cogswell encountered Irving's ghost again. As Cogswell approached the specter, it quickly faded from view, and the book the ghost had been reading fell to the floor. Eventually Cogswell related his experience to close friends, who were convinced that he needed to retreat to the country for a little rest and rejuvenation. It is ironic that the author of the first American ghost story, "The Legend of Sleepy Hollow," was also the first famous ghost of New York City. News of Washington Irving's ghost spread worldwide, as his work was well known in England, France, and Germany.

Diarist George Templeton Strong wrote that before Cogswell encountered Irving's ghost, he had also seen the spirit of Austin L. Sands, an insurance executive and merchant. Strong suggested that Cogswell had developed a comfort level with ghosts by the time he met up with Irving's spirit because of his previous spirit encounters. It should be noted that Strong was known to embellish his diary entries. Therefore, one cannot fully rely on the storytelling by Strong or his diary.

Through the years, the building changed from a private library to the home of the Hebrew Immigrant Aid Society. In fact, if you walk out the front door of the theater, turn right, and walk to the corner of the building, you can see the faded black letters HIAS near the top. In 1967, the New York Public Library, who by then owned the building, chose to lease it for a dollar a year to create the Public Theater. The columns in the main foyer reflect the original architecture of the library.

I interviewed Sam Neuman, Press Manager at the Public Theater. He explained that the scaffolding on the front of the building is in preparation for major renovations to begin in March 2010. Sam has worked at the theater for four years, and while he has not witnessed any paranormal activity personally, he said there have been reports of a female apparition in one of the second-floor theaters. Sam pointed out that the main foyer is the only way in and out of the building, and that the small size of the theaters makes it easy for an audience member or performer to realize when someone doesn't belong there or appears to be dressed in clothing of a different time period. He also mentioned that a tunnel connects the Public Theater to the building across the street.

Before Sam returned to work, I made sure he had my business card, and I cautioned him that ghostly activity could increase once the renovations ensued. Sam was kind enough to introduce me to Kenneth Leslie, security guard for the theater for over ten years. Ken knows a lot about the history of the neighborhood as well as the theater building. I asked Ken if he had any knowledge of ghosts in the theaters. He directed me to the Yeshiva Theater on the first floor. Ken said that in the back of that theater is the "Rabbi Room," and that people hear the voices of children whispering when they are alone in that room. I was able to enter the Yeshiva Theater since there was no show in progress. I took digital photos and attempted to capture EVPs. However, the background noise from people having lunch and milling around the foyer made it impossible to record properly for EVPs.

I went from the Yeshiva Theater down the hallway toward the kitchen and restrooms. I had my digital audio recorder on, just in case I might capture an EVP. The hallway was less noisy than the echoey, high-ceilinged foyer but still too noisy to discern any disembodied voices that may have been present.

Returning to the foyer, I asked Ken if he had experienced any haunting activity while working at the Public Theater. He said, without missing a beat, "I won't work here at night!" I asked him why, and he repeated emphatically that he would not want to be in the building at night. Ken then told me the story of another security guard, a friend of his, who had been alone at the theater at night and had heard the sound of a heavy chain being dragged across the floor in the basement. He went to inspect the basement but found no one there. He was so frightened, he ran upstairs and locked up for the night.

Inscribed on the ceiling beams in the foyer are the titles of various plays that have been performed at the Public Theater over the years. One that caught my eye was *Macbeth*. Given the clanking chains and disembodied laughter already present, I advise that you not read the aforementioned title aloud while in the Public Theater.

# Spotlight: Radio City Music Hall

Whether or not you celebrate Christmas, one staple fixture of the holiday season is the Christmas Show at Radio City Music Hall. The lavish production entertains and mesmerizes audiences every year. The stage is one hundred feet wide and sixty feet high, and it has three elevator sections that use hydraulic power to to raise and lower the performers and props for an added "Wow!" factor. The orchestra pit is supported by a fourth elevator which can raise and lower the entire orchestra on cue during the show. The design and engineering that went into Radio City Music Hall are remarkable even by today's standards. In fact, today's engineers have reviewed the hydraulic system and concluded there is nothing to upgrade or change.

Radio City Music Hall opened in 1932 as the largest theater in New York City. It occupied a full city block. What better way to use the piece of property, valued at $91 million, on which John D. Rockefeller had a twenty-four-year lease? Rockefeller sought the help of Samuel Lionel Rothafel to bring this theater to a profitable life in

spite of the Great Depression. "Roxy," as Rothafel was nicknamed, possessed "theatrical genius by employing an innovative combination of vaudeville, movies and razzle-dazzle decor to revive struggling theatres across America," according to Radio City's Web site. The rainbow-arched backdrop behind the stage provides the look of sunrise and sunset as seen from the deck of a ship. The balcony represents the ship's deck. There are no support columns, so every seat is a good seat in this theater.

Complementing Roxy's showmanship was the interior design talent of then-unknown Donald Deskey, who created the Grand Foyer, along with all the other smoking rooms, the lounges, and the Diamond Lobby. He used basic materials like cork, Bakelite, and aluminum to stunning effect.

My mother and I took the tour of Radio City Music Hall, which is well worth the time and money. You may take pictures, but no recording of any kind is allowed, so you won't be able to collect EVPs. I managed to capture an orb in the Grand Foyer. It might be genuine, as none of my other photos contained orbs. The tour lasts about an hour; plan to wear comfy walking shoes or sneakers, because the tour goes from the backstage hydraulics up to Roxy's suite, which includes climbing stairs and plenty of walking. At the conclusion of the tour, I decided to follow up on the ghost of Roxy story I had read about in other ghost-related books. I asked the guide if he had ever encountered the ghost of Roxy. His answer was simply, "No." In fact, he remarked that I was the first person who had ever asked him about Roxy as a ghost.

I spoke with Diane Jaust, archivist for Radio City, and she was intrigued by the story, but she said she had no information on Roxy's ghost. She went into research mode and tracked down former Rockettes and ballet dancers from the 1940s, 1950s, and 1960s. Everyone she spoke with said they never encountered his ghost, nor had they ever felt the theater was haunted. I heard from one of the former ballerinas, Janice Herbert. She said, "I called all the dancers I know who performed at Radio City, and the answer to Roxy's ghost being there was 'No,' with a lot of laughter." My inquiries had yielded nothing, but I'm glad they at least provided some entertainment.

Yet, according to Dr. Philip Schoenberg, founder and head tour guide for *Ghosts of New York Walking Tours*, Roxy has been seen at 1260 Sixth Avenue in Rockefeller Center "on opening nights . . . accompanied by a glamorous female companion." Other reports say that Roxy's ghost, along with a beautiful lady lady on his arm, has been seen walking down the aisle toward their seats, vanishing before reaching them.

Places as old and as rich in history as Radio City Music Hall typically yield some sort of residual haunting or ghost. This is one of those spots that requires the paranormal investigator to take a closer look. Raise the great curtain on the paranormal and decide for yourself.

# Hotels and Apartment Buildings

# CHAPTER 30

# Chelsea and Algonquin Hotels

THE CHELSEA HOTEL IS LOCATED between Seventh and Eighth Avenues on West 23rd Street. It's a twelve-story, red brick building that was the tallest building in New York City when it was constructed in 1883. It held onto that title until 1899. Originally an apartment cooperative, the Chelsea was converted into a hotel in 1905, having been sold to save its previous owners from bankruptcy. The hotel owes its name to Captain Thomas Clark, a veteran officer of the French and Indian Wars. Clark built his estate, which he named Chelsea, along the banks of the Hudson River in 1750.

As a hotel, the Chelsea gained a reputation as the hub for a Bohemian crowd of artists, poets, musicians, and writers. It's credited with being the birthplace of modern art. This is also the hotel in which Dylan Thomas was staying at the time of his death in 1953. Other tragically famous guests included Jimi Hendrix and Janis Joplin. Not-so-tragic guests included Bob Dylan and also Arthur C. Clarke, who wrote *2001: A Space Odyssey* while staying at the Chelsea. When Thomas Wolfe, author of *Look Homeward, Angel*, wasn't ogling female guests from his favorite room at the Grove Park Inn in Asheville, North Carolina, he stayed at the Chelsea. Wolfe's ghost has been spotted on the Chelsea's eighth floor.

Dylan Thomas' ghost has been spotted in room 206 by a guest who woke early in the morning to his ghostly face watching her from the end of the bed. Before she could fully come to grips with what she was seeing, the face slowly dissipated. However, if you're going to invest between $200 and $300 for a night's stay in hopes of experiencing the paranormal, then the room you really want to reserve is one of the two that adjoin room 100. Room 100 is where Nancy Spungen was stabbed to death on October 12, 1978, allegedly by her boyfriend, punk rocker Sid Vicious, bassist for the Sex Pistols. Sid died of a heroin overdose a year later, at the age of twenty-two, before his trial for second-degree murder. Today, guests at the Chelsea sometimes report seeing the ghost of John Simon Ritchie, a.k.a. Sid Vicious, around the first-floor elevator. Guests staying on either side of room 100 have reported hearing loud music and the sounds of a couple arguing. When the hotel management assures complaining guests that room 100 is vacant, they find it even harder to sleep.

Other ghostly activity at the Chelsea includes the sound of loud footsteps, as if someone is pacing the hallway. Of course, when irritated guests open their doors to tell the heavy-footed, inconsiderate guest to "keep it down," they find the hallway empty. Room 124 has a ghost: His identity is unknown, but he is always sighted in or near the bathroom. In various rooms, electrical malfunctions occur, lights turn themselves on and off, and faucets turn themselves on. Throughout the Chelsea, some guests have reported hearing a woman's high-pitched scream. The Star Lounge, in the basement of the Chelsea, has had issues with lights that turn on and off, as well as inexplicable noises and poltergeists rearranging furniture.

The Chelsea Hotel, with its thick walls and high ceilings, was a perfect place for musicians to practice and write their music without disturbing other guests, such as the authors who needed peace and quiet. Yet the ghosts of the Chelsea still find ways to be heard and acknowledged.

In keeping with a place to get a scary night's sleep, here is another haunted hotel. The Algonquin Hotel, located at 59 West 44th Street. The Algonquin was the first hotel in New York City to introduce smoke detectors, electronic key cards and air conditioning in all rooms. In 1919, the Edwardian-style building became home to the "Vicious Circle," a group of journalists and accomplished writers that included Dorothy Parker, Robert Benchley, Robert Sherwood, Alexander Woollcott, Harold Ross, Heywood Broun, George S. Kaufman, F. Scott Fitzgerald, Marc Connelly, and Edna Ferber. They met daily for lunch at their "Round Table" in the hotel's Rose Room. Occasionally, Douglas Fairbanks and Harpo Marx would drop by and contribute to the group's scintillating conversations.

Dorothy Parker founded this group and on most days was the only female in attendance. Armed with her razor-sharp wit, Parker could easily deflate an ego or two without missing a beat. However, she had a depressing childhood: her parents had died when she was very young, and her brother died aboard the *Titanic*. Some of that inner darkness came out in Parker's poems, such as "I Shall Come Back." Her best-known lines are probably "Men seldom make passes at girls who wear glasses" and "Brevity is the soul of lingerie." With her husband, Alan Campbell, Parker co-wrote the script for *A Star Is Born*. In spite of two suicide attempts, she died of natural causes on June 6, 1967, at the age of seventy-three.

Shortly after Parker died, strange things began to happen at the Algonquin Hotel. The staff noticed objects that went missing and then reappeared, and dressing tables that rearranged themselves. It makes sense that Dorothy would return to a place where she was happiest. Guests at the Algonquin have reported hearing furniture moving at all hours of the night and an elevator that behaves erratically.

The Vicious Circle may still be meeting daily in the afterlife of the Algonquin. Guests and staff report seeing shadows from the corners of their eyes. Sometimes a full-body apparition resembling Dorothy Parker is seen whisking through the lobby or down a hallway and vanishing. On New Year's Eve, the hotel staff have a tradition of entering the lobby precisely at midnight and banging pots and pans as loud as they can to ward off any negative spirits for the upcoming year.

That tradition did not prevent the suicide of the multitalented Susannah McCorkle, who sang her jazz-pop songs woven together as stories in the Oak Room of the Algonquin. In May 2001, McCorkle jumped to her death from her apartment building on West 86th Street. She was distraught over the cancellation of her contract at the Algonquin. She left behind a suicide note and a will that detailed how her estate was to be handled. She was only fifty-five years old at the time of her death. Her friends and family couldn't understand why she had taken the Algonquin's contract cancellation so hard.

Her obituary in the *New York Times* stated, "With a repertory of more than 3,000 songs and with seventeen albums to her credit, Ms. McCorkle was more than a nightclub singer. She was a passionate, intrepid scholar of 20th-century pop. And her cabaret shows, which she wrote herself, featured rich anecdotal histories of the songwriters whose work she performed. Her honors included three *Album of the Year* awards from Stereo Review." A highly intelligent woman who spoke five languages fluently in addition to being an award-winning short-story writer, McCorkle easily could have moved on to another performance venue or resumed work as an interpreter. Perhaps she succumbed to a dark curse fostered by the depression of Dorothy Parker. Both were female writers and overachievers whose childhoods had been nomadic. (McCorkle's father was an anthropologist who traveled around the country to present his research at various colleges.)

Cursed or not, the Algonquin hotel clearly has guests who have checked in for the long haul. It's also in a prime location for visitors to "the Big Apple," as it's within walking distance of the theater district and the Empire State Building. If you're a fan of insomnia as well as ghosthunting, then you should definitely book a room at either the Chelsea or the Algonquin.

# CHAPTER 31

# The Dakota

THE DAKOTA IS A FAMOUS upper-west-side apartment building where the rich and famous reside. Construction began in 1880 at the direction of Edward Clark, the founding partner and president of the Singer Sewing Machine company. Clark was a lawyer by profession, but he invested money in the risky business of real estate to grow his financial portfolio. When he began construction of a luxury apartment building, people called it "Clark's Folly" and joked that it was so far from the epicenter of Manhattan, it might as well have been in the Dakota Territory. That joke led to the name of the building. Clark died in 1882, two years before the Dakota's completion, with an estimated net worth of approximately $20 million.

Clark was a risk-taker and a visionary in the way he adapted and upgraded tenement living for the wealthy. Thanks to the innovative "donut" design, a central courtyard with the building all around it, each apartment got a view of the courtyard, and all tenants enjoyed its privacy, as the only entrance to the courtyard was via a gated doorway that had a doorman on duty at all times. Another way Clark marketed his apartments to affluent tenants was by including shared amenities, such as a dining room, store-rooms, laundry facilities, a bake shop, and a wine cellar. The Dakota also had its own power plant, extra servants' quarters, playrooms, a gymnasium, and tennis courts. However, the key selling point was the Dakota's multiple elevators, which ensured that no matter which of the sixty-five apartments one rented, there would be no need to break a sweat climbing to one's abode. Before the building officially opened in 1884, all the apartments were rented.

The façade of the Dakota is a blend of German Gothic, French Renaissance, and English Victorian architectural styles. It was the perfect backdrop for Roman Polanski's 1968 thriller *Rosemary's Baby*. It should be noted that only the outside shots in that movie were filmed on location at the Dakota; no filming is allowed inside the building in deference to the strict policy protecting tenants' privacy.

However, no privacy policy is strong enough to keep the ghosts of the Dakota from appearing to tenants and their visi-tors. Paula Santangelo was quoted in a *New York Times* article about her encounter: "In 1982, I was waiting for a friend in an apartment on the 10th floor. He was an accompanist for opera singers and was there for a rehearsal. As I waited in the foyer, a little girl dressed in period clothing, later it occurred to me she was dressed in what I could only term as 'turn of the century garb,' suddenly appeared, smiled at me and disappeared into an adjoining room, which was later pointed out to be a closet. The

**The front entrance to the Dakota, where John Lennon was murdered.**
**(Photo by Grace Agnew)**

apartment's resident informed me that I had seen the 'resident ghost', a young girl possibly 10 to 12 years of age. To this day I can clearly picture her in detail. Obviously an experience I will never forget!"

Over the years, this little girl ghost has appeared to people in the building at various times. Usually people describe her as wearing a yellow taffeta dress and say that she stops bouncing her red ball long enough to tearfully say, "Today is my birthday." Supposedly, seeing this sad little ghost is a bad omen, usually foreshadowing the impending death of the witness.

The ghost of the building's original owner and builder, Edward Clark, shows up occasionally. One time he reportedly shook his toupee violently at workmen in the basement of the building. Another time, he appeared ever so briefly to an electrician working in the basement. Later, when the electrician saw a picture of Edward Clark, he realized he had seen Clark's ghost.

Boris Karloff, the actor who famously portrayed the monster in the movie *Frankenstein,* had an apartment in the basement of the Dakota, yet he doesn't haunt the place. It's possible that the disappointment of hanging a bag of candy outside his door for trick-or-treaters on Halloween only to have the candy go untouched had something to do with Karloff's "moving on." Apparently, Karloff's monster role was enough to keep the children away—even from candy.

In 1975, John and Yoko Ono Lennon moved into the Dakota, purchasing an apartment formerly owned by actor Robert Ryan. Ryan's wife, Jessie, had died in the apartment, but she was not about to relinquish her stay just because she was dead. The Lennons knew early on that their apartment was haunted, and in 1979, they called in a psychic to conduct a séance. Mrs. Ryan came through and politely informed John and Yoko that she was not leaving her apartment. John was open to spirituality and otherworldly topics, so he was comfortable coexisting with the spirit of Mrs. Ryan.

Although it would have made for a chilling story to say that John Lennon saw the ghost of the sad little girl on December 7, 1980, he didn't. At a different time, he did see the spirit of a crying woman who walked down the hall and vanished. This "crying lady ghost" has been witnessed by other Dakota residents over the years, too.

The most shocking and devastating event in the Dakota's history happened on December 8, 1980, when Mark David Chapman gunned down John Lennon as he and Yoko were returning from a late-night recording session. Chapman called out, "Mr. Lennon," and before John could turn around, Chapman fired five shots from a .38 caliber revolver into John's back. Within minutes, police arrived on the scene to find John dying in Yoko's arms as Chapman sat calmly off to the side reading *The Catcher in the Rye.* The debate rages on as to whether or not John Lennon haunts the Dakota.

The Strawberry Fields Memorial (Photo by Grace Agnew)

In 1983, Joey Harrow, a musician, and Amanda Moores, a writer, both saw the ghost of John Lennon standing at the entrance of the Dakota. Joey described the ghost as having an eerie glow around him. Amanda said she wanted to talk to the ghost but sensed by the way John's spirit looked at her that she had better not approach him. Additionally, over the years people have reported seeing John's ghost around the Strawberry Fields memorial to John, located in Central Park.

Surely the most reliable and believable sighting of John Lennon's ghost comes from his wife, Yoko. She saw him seated at his piano in their apartment. He looked at her and said, "Don't be afraid, I am still with you."

Another ghost spotted at the Dakota was that of a ten-year-old boy, seen in 1965 by several people in apartment 77. The boy slowly walked down the hallway between two bedrooms and disappeared from sight. Witnesses reported an unpleasant out-doorsy-musty odor accompanying this specter.

Poltergeist activity at the Dakota includes elevators that start and stop for no apparent reason, and lights that turn themselves on or off. Trash bags have levitated, and several small fires have mysteriously started. In another strange incident, a tenant approaching the Dakota looked up at his apartment and saw a beautiful, brightly lit chandelier in his living-room window—which was a strange thing to see because he didn't have a chandelier. During some repair work a few months later, he discovered the nub of a light fixture that would have had a chandelier suspended from it.

My friend and fellow ghosthunter Grace Agnew has visited the Dakota and Strawberry Fields. She told me, "Although I am not a strong believer in orbs, there is a clear orb at the Dakota in my shot at the entrance with the doorman, up toward the top and to the right. I wanted to photograph the entrance since that is where John Lennon was shot." Grace is an experienced paranormal investigator and follows protocols much like those the NJGHS sets forth to distinguish between false-positive orbs and genuine ones; therefore, I trust the validity of her orb photo.

Across from the Dakota is Central Park. Beyond the Strawberry Fields memorial on the southeast end of the park is Wollman Rink. This ice-skating rink was a favorite of the Van der Vroot sisters, Janet and Rosetta, in the mid-1800s. During the winter months the two sisters skated all day, taking a break only for lunch at Delmonico's. The rest of the year, the sisters were most unhappy and argued with each other constantly. They simply loved and lived to be on the ice at Wollman Rink, doing their figure-eights. In 1880, a gala event was held on the ice of Wollman Rink, complete with fireworks, for Janet's thirty-fifth birthday. Janet wore a stunning outfit of dark purple velvet, and Rosetta wore an equally stunning outfit of green satin and red velvet. The sisters were always inseparable and never married. They died in 1915 within three months of each other. By World War I, people visiting the rink reported seeing two young ladies, one in purple velvet and one in red velvet, skating beautifully on the ice. At first it was only suspected that these young women on the ice were phantom apparitions; once the summer months arrived and people still saw the two girls skating above the water, the ghost sightings were confirmed.

The American Museum of Natural History is only a few blocks away from the Dakota. Therefore, you can make a very full day of visiting the Dakota, Central Park, and Wollman Rink. Perhaps you'll see the Van der Vroot sisters ice-skating or John Lennon leaning up against the entrance of the Dakota. In any event, make sure you take plenty of pictures.

CHAPTER 32

# Fordham University

FORDHAM UNIVERSITY, the Jesuit University of New York, has a beautiful campus located in the Bronx close to the New York Botanical Garden and the famous Bronx Zoo. Fordham was established in 1841 as St. John's College on Rose Hill Manor, which was at that time part of Westchester County. In 1907, the name was changed to Fordham University. According to the university's Web site, "the name Fordham is derived from the Anglo-Saxon words 'ford' and 'ham,' meaning a wading place or ford by a settlement." Today approximately 3,800 students reside on campus.

If you visit the campus, make sure you have comfortable walking shoes; the visitor parking is located near the entrance, while the buildings you'll want to see are across the campus.

Fordham is probably one of the most haunted universities in the United States; there are at least six actively haunted buildings on the Rose Hill campus. I have included a campus map on which these buildings are indicated by shaded oval markings.

I visited Fordham in February 2010, and my first stop was Queen's Court to check out a story I heard from Roberto Soto when I visited the Nautical Museum on City Island. Roberto had attended a presentation at Fordham given by Thomas Casey, an author and lecturer on ghosts and the paranormal. The story that Casey related dates back to 2003. It was summer, and the resident assistants (RAs) were cleaning out the halls of the dormitories to prepare for the incoming freshmen.

The St. Robert's wing of Queen's Court, built in 1940, had a room on the first floor that was presenting a challenge to the RAs. Every time they went into this room, they found the mattresses removed from the beds and standing upright against the wall. Initially they dismissed it as a prank by fellow RAs from either Bishop's or St. John's Halls, the other buildings that make up Queen's Court, and they replaced the mattresses. After several separate inspections, each of which ended with the discovery that the mattresses had again been placed against the wall, the St. Robert's RAs were no longer amused. They fixed the mattresses once more and then locked the room. An hour later, they returned to look and were horrified to find the mattresses once again standing against the wall.

Later that night, the RA who had locked the door and kept the key with him was awakened by the sound of knocking on his door. He stumbled out of bed and answered the door. A kindly Jesuit priest told the young man that someone must have been praying pretty hard to have him up at this hour. He went on to say that "it" usually stays in the room at the end of the hall but had escaped. The priest assured the young man that he had "taken care of it." The priest left, and the young man returned to his bed and went back to sleep.

The next morning, the RA went to the office to thank the nun whom he figured had sent the priest to him the night before. The nun said she had not dispatched any priest and did not know of any Jesuit fitting the description the RA gave her.

Is it possible a ghost priest exorcised a poltergeist from St. Robert's Hall? Or was the ghost priest the spirit of another Jesuit who allegedly hanged himself in one of the dormitory halls? The thudding of his dangling feet against the radiator is a sound mentioned by RAs to terrorize incoming freshmen. Of course, the banging could easily be explained by the expansion and contraction of the pipes conducting the heat to the radiators. However, it could also be the result of another ghost said to haunt O'Hare Hall. During the construction of O'Hare Hall, one of the workers lost his life, and it's believed that he hasn't missed a day's work in spite of his death. He keeps banging on the walls as if he is still constructing the building.

While I was walking around Queen's Court, I met a young female Fordham student who told me about Hughes Hall. She said that scenes from the original movie *The Exorcist* were filmed there. Of course, I went right over. As some students were exiting Hughes, I stopped them to inquire about the paranormal activity. One of them said that he had heard about the ghost of a little boy who has been seen late at night, but he said he had never witnessed this ghost personally. This claim is also mentioned on the Web site Unexplainable.net: "During the wee hours of the night, some students claim the ghost of a young boy who appears in the rooms visits them. Locked doors have also swung open on their own in Hughes Hall."

Finlay Hall is a former medical school building that now serves as a dormitory. Students there have reported being grabbed by the throat and choked in the middle of the night.

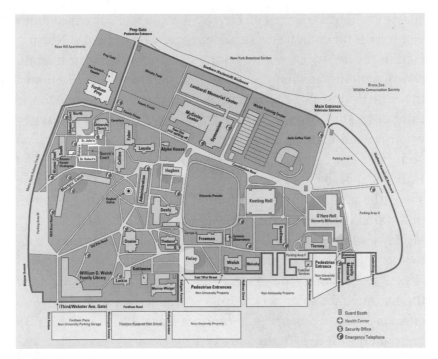

**Fordham University Rose Hill Campus map**

Doors slam, and furniture is moved by unseen hands, sometimes accompanied by a child's laughter.

The dorm at Martyr's Court has two known ghosts. A blonde-
haired ghost girl has been seen standing in the shower, just staring blankly ahead. The ghost of an unidentified man is seen
walking down the hall past the dorm rooms. When a student
catches a glimpse of this man and tries to follow him, he simply
vanishes. Children's laughter seems to come from the walls of
Martyr's Court as well.

Keating Hall is one of the more recently constructed buildings on campus. It was built over the original morgue tunnels
from the 1930s. After a new cafeteria was built, the basement of
Keating Hall was converted to a library. I found the energy here

charged with paranormal electricity; I could feel it the moment I entered the room. In fact, a security guard who worked at Keating Hall in the late 1970s was so frightened by doors slamming and chairs banging against the walls that he quit. Students report the eerie feeling of being watched while on the first floor. On the third floor, students may feel a hand clamped on their shoulders when no one is there. Darting shadows and vague apparitions seen from the corner of one's eye are commonplace at Keating Hall. Inexplicable cold spots have been reported on the staircase above the auditorium. One student saw a chair tumble down this staircase when no one else was around.

My visit to Fordham University was fruitless in terms of capturing any evidence of paranormal activity, but I was impressed at how forthcoming the students were with their insights as to the haunted hot spots on campus. I wonder if the ghosts were either auditing or sleeping through a class that day, saving up their energy for the "night shift."

# Spotlight: Various Ghosts of New York City

Just like the living, ghosts come in all different shapes, sizes and personalities. Most people are frightened when they encounter a ghost. It is, after all, out of the norm to see through a person or witness someone disappearing through a wall. Like anything else intimidating, once you've been exposed to it enough, it becomes less frightening. Over the years I've investigated many cases in private homes where, once the identity of the ghost is discovered, the homeowner feels more comfortable and is open to the idea of coexisting with a spirit.

Some ghosts can be violent or malevolent depending on the circumstances at the time of their deaths. Typically, ghosts of people who died by beheading are the most violent, as the last thing they recall at the moment of death is sheer anger over losing their heads. The "Old Moor" ghost of Clinton Court, located at 422½ West 46th Street and Tenth Avenue, is said to be a ghost one should avoid. He did not die by beheading; rather, the former sailor was hanged for mutiny aboard a ship that was bound for New York in the early eighteenth century. His body was buried in an unmarked grave in a potter's field that, a hundred years later, became known as "Hell's Kitchen." The Old Moor gained a companion in the nineteenth century when a curious young lady went looking for the famous ghost. Upon encountering him, she was so frightened that she tripped over her dress while running, fell down the iron stairs, and died. There are two versions of her story. Both versions say that she was pregnant at the time of her death and the baby was rescued. One version, however, adds the baby was a girl who, as a young child, liked to pretend to be a ghost by running around the courtyard with a sheet over her head. Supposedly she tripped on the sheet and fell, becoming the third ghost to join the "Clinton Court Crew." Yet another story says that a different little girl had an encounter with the Old Moor that caused her to fall from a balcony to her death.

Then there are those ghosts who need to have their story heard in order to be released. Such was the case of "Hungry Lucy," who pounded on the walls of 428 West 44th Street at all hours of the night in the 1950s and 1960s, preventing actress June Havoc from having a peaceful night's sleep. June eventually met Hans Holzer at the suggestion of one of her television show's viewers. Holzer brought with him the psychic medium Sybil Leek. After a couple of séances at June's house with Sybil, the identity of the ghost came to light: one Lucy Ryan who had lived there in 1792.

As channeled by Sybil, Lucy fell in love with one of the Continental Army's soldiers and promised to wait for him to return from maneuvers in New Jersey. Food was scarce, and whatever food was to be had always went to the soldiers first. Lucy spent most of her days without food, hence her nickname "Hungry Lucy." One night, Lucy was brutally attacked and raped by some drunken soldiers. She was injured so badly she was unable to seek help, and she later died.

June Havoc suspected that Lucy was buried in a small area of her backyard where nothing ever grew despite her repeated attempts to plant things there. The nights that followed the revelation of Lucy were marked with increased noises: banging, tapping and shrill screams. Finally, things quieted down. Lucy must have moved on, having accepted the fact that she had long since died.

Warfare, of course, creates many ghosts. Believe it or not, there is a World War II ghost in midtown Manhattan at the Empire State Building. Before they installed higher, jump-proof barriers on the building's observation deck, the Empire State Building had been the best place in the city to take that last big step. The ghosts of past jumpers are seen here late at night. One in particular is also seen in the ladies' restroom. She is about twenty years old and dressed in 1940s garb. She applies bright red lipstick to her lips as she mutters about how she and her fiancé were childhood sweethearts and were going to get married. This same young lady ghost is seen on the observation deck, where she announces that her fiancé was killed in the war, then runs to the edge of the deck and somehow jumps off in spite of the safety barrier. Women who have seen this ghostly suicide think they're hallucinating and retreat to the ladies restroom to gain their composure. There, they encounter the ghost once more, applying her lipstick.

There are also possessive ghosts, which are dangerous in that they can wear a living person down and take possession of him. Sometimes they choose a person who is already worn down through substance abuse and/or mental illness. Once they have possession of the person, the ghost can relive its torture on the new victim. A good example of this may be the ghost at 14 West Tenth Street, where Mark Twain once resided. Some people suspect that Twain haunts the stairwell of the Victorian apartment house, but the example of a possessive ghost is what I think prevails here. According to Dennis William Hauck, author of *Haunted Places*, prior to World War II, two immigrants living in this building tortured their child by making the youngster walk around in circles for hours while tied to a rope looped over the top of a chair. The young child eventually succumbed to starvation. Were these parents the victims of a possessive, malicious spirit already present in the building? Or were they the embodiment of evil, whose negative energy remained long after they died?

Joel Steinberg, who lived in a third-floor apartment in this building, beat his adopted six-year-old daughter Elizabeth ("Lisa") to death on November 2, 1987. Is it possible that the sick, abusive energies of the immigrant parents from the past took possession of the current residents, forcing them to inflict unspeakable abuse upon innocent children? I am not offering this theory in any way to defend what Steinberg did, nor to relieve him of accountability in Lisa's murder. From a supernatural standpoint, though, there is a macabre pattern here that a paranormal investigator has to examine and consider further.

Some ghosts prove to be helpful, as in the case of the "cleaning ghost" who dwells in an apartment at an undisclosed address in New York City. I heard this story years ago from Jane Doherty, who was then the President of the Jersey Society of Parapsychology. In the 1980s, a young "power couple" moved into an apartment shortly after their marriage. They both worked full-time jobs and therefore were out of the apartment the better part of each weekday. The wife would come home from work and find the mail piled neatly on the coffee table and the dish towel hanging nicely over the handle of the oven door. Since they had a mail slot in the door, and normally the mail would be strewn all over the floor upon its delivery, she figured her husband must have come home during his lunch break and tidied up. There were also days when the wife worked late and the husband returned home before her to find the mail neatly piled and the kitchen all tidy. He figured that his wife had come home at lunch, even though it wouldn't have been convenient for her to do so, due to her commute.

One day the wife left work early and figured she'd have time at home to make a nice dinner and surprise her husband. When she got home, she was surprised because he, too, had left work early. Happy to see her, the husband suggested they take a nice walk and enjoy dinner at a restaurant. She was thrilled and thanked him for being so thoughtful and always placing the mail on the coffee table. He stopped dead in his tracks and looked at her and said, "I thought that was you putting it there." She explained, as he already knew, how ridiculous it would be for her to make the commute home just for lunch. They decided to conduct a test. They scattered the mail all over the floor and removed the dish towel from the oven door handle, leaving it on the kitchen floor. Then they left for their walk and dinner. When they returned, the mail was piled neatly on the coffee table and the dish towel was hanging perfectly the handle of the oven door. They ran this test several more times, each time concluding with the same results. If you're like me, you're thinking, "I can't even get my kids to take out the trash. How does one score a cleaning ghost?"

# Visiting Haunted Sites

### Alice Austen House    (718) 816-4506

2 Hylan Boulevard, Staten Island, NY 10305
www.aliceausten.org

**Hours:** Open all year except January, February, and major holidays. Grounds
are open every day until dusk. Home is open Thursday–Sunday, noon–5 P.M.
**Admission:** Suggested donation of $2 per person.

### Algonquin Hotel    (212) 840-6800

59 West 44th Street (between Fifth and Sixth Avenues), New York, NY 10036
www.algonquinhotel.com

### Belasco Theater    (212) 239-6200

111 West 44th Street, New York, NY 10036
www.shubertorganization.com

### Bridge Café    (212) 227-3344

279 Water Street, New York, NY 10038
www.bridgecafenyc.com

### Brooklyn Inn    (718) 522-2525

148 Hoyt Street, Brooklyn, NY 11217

**Hours:** Monday–Thursday, 4 P.M.–4 A.M.; Friday, 3 P.M.–4 A.M.; Saturday and
Sunday, 2 P.M.–4 A.M.

### Chelsea Hotel    (212) 243-3700

222 West 23rd Street (between Seventh and Eighth Avenues), New York, NY
10011
www.hotelchelsea.com

### Cherry Lane Theater    (212) 989-2020

38 Commerce Street, New York, NY 10014
www.cherrylanetheatre.com

## Conference House    (718) 984-6046

298 Satterlee Street, Staten Island, NY 10307
www.conferencehouse.org

**Hours:** April to mid-December, Friday–Sunday, 1–4 P.M.
**Admission:** $3 adults; $2 children and seniors
There is free parking at the visitor center, located at the end of Hylan Boulevard.

## The Dakota

One West 72nd Street, New York, NY 10023

## Ear Inn    (212) 226-9060

326 Spring Street, New York, NY 10013

Lunch and dinner are served daily; brunch is available on Sundays.

## Ellis and Liberty Islands    (877) 523-9849

via Statue Cruises
**Mailing address:** Statue Cruises, 1 Audrey Zapp Drive, Jersey City, NJ 07305
**Ferry terminals:** Located in Battery Park (NYC) and Liberty State Park (NJ).

**Tour and ferry schedules:** www.statuecruises.com/ferry-service/schedule-options.aspx
**Tickets:** Purchase online at www.statuecruises.com, by phone at the number above, or at either terminal.

## Fordham University    (718) 817-1000

441 East Fordham Road, Bronx, NY 10458
www.fordham.edu

For Rose Hill Campus maps and directions, see www.fordham.edu/discover_
fordham/where_is_fordham/maps__directions/rose_hill_directions

## Fort Wadsworth (718) 354-4500

East end of Bay Street, Staten Island, NY
www.statenislandusa.com/pages/ft_wadsworth.html

**Hours:** The visitor center is open Wednesday–Sunday, 10 A.M.–4:30 P.M.
Ranger-led tours are free and depart the visitor center at 2:30 P.M.

### Garibaldi-Meucci Museum     (718) 442-1608

420 Tompkins Avenue, Staten Island, NY 10305
www.garibaldimeuccimuseum.org

Hours: Tuesday–Friday, 1–5 P.M.
Admission: $5

### Manhattan Bistro     (212) 966-3459

129 Spring Street, New York, NY 10012

### McSorley's Ale House     (212) 473-9148

15 East Seventh Street, New York, NY 10003
www.mcsorleysnewyork.com

**Hours:** Monday–Saturday, 11 A.M.–1 A.M.; Sunday, 1 P.M.–1 A.M.

### Merchant's House Museum     (212) 777-1089

29 East Fourth Street, New York, NY 10003
www.merchantshouse.org

**Hours:** Thursday–Monday, noon–5 P.M. Closed Tuesdays and
Wednesdays. Closed on Easter, Independence Day, Thanksgiving Day, Christmas
Eve, Christmas Day, and New Year's Eve.
**Admission:** $10 general, $5 students/seniors; free for members and for
children under age 12 accompanied by an adult.
Tours are self-guided, with docents available to answer questions. To arrange a
group tour, see www.merchantshouse.org/visit/groups.php

### Morris-Jumel Mansion     (212) 923-8008

65 Jumel Terrace, New York, NY 10032
www.morrisjumel.org

**Hours:** Wednesday–Sunday, 10 A.M.–4 P.M. Monday and Tuesday by
appointment only.
**Admission:** $5 adults, $4 seniors and students, free for children ages 12 and
under with an adult. The museum is closed on New Year's Day, Memorial Day,
Independence Day, Labor Day, Thanksgiving, and Christmas.

### New Amsterdam Theater     (212) 282-2900

214 West 42nd Street, New York, NY 10036
www.newamsterdamtheatre.net

Call for show tickets.

## Old Bermuda Inn   (718) 948-7600

301 Veterans Road West, Staten Island, NY 10309
Mailing address: 2512 Arthur Kill Road, Staten Island, NY 10309
www.theoldbermudainn.com

For information about the Wedding Cottage Bed and Breakfast, see www.
theoldbermudainn.com/Bed-and-Breakfast.html

## One If By Land, Two If By Sea   (212) 255-8649

17 Barrow Street, New York, NY 10014
www.oneifbyland.com

Hours: Monday–Thursday, 5:3010 P.M.; Friday and Saturday, 5:15–11:15
P.M.; Sunday brunch, 11:30 A.M.–2 P.M.; Sunday dinner, 5:30–9:30 P.M.

## Palace Theater   (212) 730-8200

1564 Broadway, New York, NY 10036
Nederlander Company: (212) 840-5577
www.palacetheaternewyork.com

## Paradise Theater   (718) 220-1015

2403 Grand Concourse, Bronx, NY 10468
www.paradisetheaterevents.com

## Public Theater   (212) 539-8500

425 Lafayette Street, New York, NY 10003
www.publictheater.org

## Radio City Music Hall

1260 Avenue of the Americas (6th Avenue), New York, NY 10020

**Box office/Radio City Avenue Store:** (212) 307-7171. Located between 50th
and 51st Streets; open daily, 11:30 A.M.–6 P.M.
**Tour information:** (212) 247-4777
**Tour prices:** $17 adults, $14 seniors, $10 children under age 12.

The Stage Door Tour is a one-hour walking tour of the interior of Radio City
Music Hall. Tours depart from the lobby about every half-hour Monday through
Saturday between 11 A.M. and 3 P.M. No tours on Sundays. Same-day tour tickets
are sold at the Radio City Avenue Store. Advance tickets for tours on future
dates are sold only at the box office or through Ticketmaster.

## Richmond Town    (718) 351-1611

441 Clarke Avenue, Staten Island, NY 10306
www.historicrichmondtown.org

**Hours:** Wednesday–Sunday, 1–5 P.M.
**Tours:** Wednesday–Friday at 2:30 P.M.; Saturday and Sunday at 2 P.M. and 3:30
P.M. Call (718) 351-1611 ext. 280 for more information. Closed on Easter Sunday,
Thanksgiving, Christmas, and New Year's Day.

## Snug Harbor    (718) 448-2500

1000 Richmond Terrace, Staten Island, NY 10301
www.snug-harbor.org

**Hours:** Grounds are open from dawn to dusk. Galleries, gardens, and gift shop
are open Tuesday–Sunday, 10 A.M.–4 P.M.
**Admission:** Adults $6 gardens and galleries, $5 for gardens only, $3 for
galleries only. Discounts for members, seniors, students, and children under
age 12; see www.snug-harbor.org/visit.html for options and rates.
**Tours:** Maps with self-guided tour information are available at Main Hall
Building C and the Gift Shop. Tours with a dedicated guide are available for an
additional $4 per person (25-person maximum.) Additional guides are retained
for groups exceeding 25 people.  Guided tours of the art galleries are available by
reservation only for groups of 15 or more.

## St. Mark's in-the-Bowery    (212) 674-6377

131 East Tenth Street, New York, NY 10003
www.stmarksbowery.org

*Services:* Sundays at 11 A.M.
Holy Eucharist & Evening Prayers: Wednesdays at 6:30 P.M.
Noon Day Prayers: Fridays at noon

## St. Paul's Chapel    (212) 233-4164

Broadway and Fulton Streets, New York, NY
www.trinitywallstreet.org/congregation/spc

*Chapel hours:* Weekdays, 10 A.M.–6 P.M.; Saturday, 10 A.M.–4 P.M.; Sunday,
7 A.M.–3 p..m.
*Churchyard hours:* Monday–Saturday, 10 A.M.–4 P.M.;* Sunday,7 A.M.–3:30 P.M.
* *Weather permitting. During Daylight Savings Time, churchyard
remains open until 5:30pm.*

Those attending Sunday services may park from 9 A.M.–5 P.M. at the Battery Parking Garage on Greenwich Street at a discounted rate of $7.

## Times Square

www.timessquarenyc.org

## Trinity Episcopal Church and Graveyard    (212) 602-0800

Broadway at Wall Street, New York, NY
www.trinitywallstreet.org

*Church hours:* Weekdays, 7 A.M.–6 P.M.; Saturday, 8 A.M.–4 P.M.; Sunday, 7 A.M.–4 P.M.
*Churchyard hours:* Weekdays, 7 A.M.–4 P.M.;* Saturdays and holidays, 8 A.M.– 3 P.M.; Sunday, 7 A.M.–3 P.M.
*Cemetery and mausoleum hours:* Daily, 9 A.M.–4 P.M.
Office open Monday–Friday only.
*\*Weather permitting. When daylight-saving time begins in spring, the churchyard remains open until 5 P.M.*

## Van Cortlandt House    (718) 543-3344

Van Cortland Park at 244th Street, New York, NY
www.vancortlandthouse.org

Note: Cars are not permitted in Van Cortlandt Park without prior arrangement. Please call Van Cortlandt House Museum if you need special assistance. Metered parking on 244th Street is available.

## "Various Ghosts of New York City" spotlight, locations mentioned in

Clinton Court: 422½ West 46th Street at Tenth Avenue

Hungry Lucy: 428 West 44th Street

Mark Twain/Ghost Possession house: 14 West Tenth Street

## Washington Square Park

Between Fifth Avenue, Waverly Place, West Fourth Street, and MacDougal Street
www.nycgovparks.org/parks/washingtonsquarepark
**Map:** www.nycgovparks.org/parks/M098-02/map

## White Horse Tavern     (212) 989-3956

(not to be confused with Whitehorse Tavern at 25 Bridge Street)
567 Hudson Street (between West 11th and Perry Streets), New York, NY 10014

The tavern offers lunch and dinner daily, brunch on Saturday and Sunday. Cash only; no credit cards accepted.

## Woodlawn Cemetery     (718) 920-0500

501 East 233rd Street at Webster Avenue, Bronx, NY 10470
Hours: Daily, 8:30 A.M.–5 P.M. (Office is closed on Sundays.)

# Bibliography

Thank you to the many proprietors, guards, bartenders, waitresses, docents, and others who so graciously granted interviews, as well as to the authors of the following works.

## Chapter 1: Bridge Café

### Books

Langan-Schmidt, Therese, *Ghosts of New York City* (Atglen, PA: Schiffer Publishing, 2003), 113–114.

Revai, Cheri, *Haunted New York: Ghosts and Strange Phenomena of the Empire State* (Mechanicsburg, PA: Stackpole Books, 2005), 86–87.

### Articles

Dwyer, Kevin, "Blasts From the Past," *New York Magazine* (June 5, 2005). www.nymag.com/nymetro/nightlife/barbuzz/11924.

Kusnyer, Laura, "Haunted New York" (October 21, 2009), www.nycgo.com/?event=view.slideshow&sid=208177&slide=3.

### Other Web pages

www.bridgecafenyc.com/Tavern_Cafe_Restaurant_New_York/?Ghost_Stories

www.bridgecafenyc.com/Tavern_Cafe_Restaurant_New_York/?The_History

## Chapter 3: Ear Inn

### Books

Revai, Cheri, *Haunted New York: Ghosts and Strange Phenomena of the Empire State* (Mechanicsburg, PA: Stackpole Books, 2005), 90–91.

### Articles

Firestone, David, "Public Lives; Man With a History, in a House With a Past," *New York Times* (October 14, 1998). www.nytimes.com/1998/10/14/nyregion/public-lives-man-with-a-history-in-a-house-with-a-past.html

Miller, Bryan, "In Hard Times, Just Plain Bars Are Timeless," *New York Times* (March 13, 1992). www.nytimes.com/1992/03/13/arts/in-hard-times-just-plain-bars-are-timeless.html.

"The Ear Inn," New York Daily Photo blog (October 22, 2009). http://newyorkdailyphoto.blogspot.com/2009/10/ear-inn.html.

"What the Guidebooks Won't Tell You," *Time Out New York* (Issue 631, November 1–7, 2007). http://newyork.timeout.com/articles/features/23933/what-the-guidebooks-wont-tell-you/17.html

**Other Web pages**

www.earinn.com

# Chapter 4: Manhattan Bistro

**Books**

Adams III, Charles, *New York City Ghost Stories* (Reading, PA: Exeter House Books, 1996), 113–121.

Revai, Cheri, *Haunted New York: Ghosts and Strange Phenomena of the Empire State* (Mechanicsburg, PA: Stackpole Books, 2005), 81–83.

**Articles**

"Answers About Haunted New York," *New York Times* City Room blog (October 29, 2007). http://cityroom.blogs.nytimes.com/2007/10/29/answers-about-haunted-new-york.

Patronite, Rob, and Robin Raisfeld, review of Manhattan Bistro, *New York Magazine*. www.nymag.com/listings/restaurant/manhattan-bistro.

Reader reviews of Manhattan Bistro, *New York Magazine*. www.nymag.com/urr/listings/restaurant/manhattan-bistro/?sort=recent.

**Other Web pages**

"The Dakota," www.nyc-architecture.com/UWS/UWS017.htm

## Chapter 5: McSorley's Ale House

### Articles

Parnell, Sean, review of McSorley's Old Ale House for the Chicago Bar Project. www.chibarproject.com/Reviews/McSorley's/McSorley's.htm.

### Other Web pages

www.mcsorleysnewyork.com/history_time_02.html

## Chapter 6: Old Bermuda Inn

### Books

Blackhall, Susan, *Ghosts of New York* (San Diego, Calif.: Thunder Bay Press, 2005), 102–105.

Revai, Cheri, *Haunted New York: Ghosts and Strange Phenomena of the Empire State* (Mechanicsburg, PA: Stackpole Books, 2005), 83.

### Web pages

"The Old Bermuda Inn," www.realhaunts.com/united-states/the-old-bermuda-inn/#comments.

### Other

Old Bermuda Inn, *The History* (flyer).

## Chapter 7: One If By Land Two If By Sea Restaurant

### Books

Blackhall, Susan, *Ghosts of New York* (San Diego, Calif.: Thunder Bay Press, 2005), 42–47.

Côté, Richard N., *Theodosia Burr Alston: Portrait of a Prodigy* (Mt. Pleasant, SC: Corinthian, 2002). Excerpts at www.bookdoctor.com/corinthian/cote/theodosia.html.

Revai, Cheri, *Haunted New York: Ghosts and Strange Phenomena of the Empire State* (Mechanicsburg, PA: Stackpole Books, 2005), 83–85.

### Articles

"City Haunts: A Ghostly Guide," *New York Times* (October 29, 1995). www. nytimes.com/1995/10/29/nyregion/city-haunts-a-ghostly-guide.html.

### Other Web pages

www.aaronburrassociation.org/richmond_hill.htm

www.legendsofamerica.com/GH-CelebrityGhosts.html

www.oldandsold.com/articles14/new-york-23.shtml

www.oneifbyland.com

# Chapter 8: White Horse Tavern

### Books

Blackhall, Susan, *Ghosts of New York* (San Diego, Calif.: Thunder Bay Press, 2005), 58–61.

### Web pages

"Poetry Landmark: The White Horse Tavern in New York City," Academy of American Poets. www.poets.org/viewmedia.php/prmMID/5747.

# Chapter 9: St. Mark's in-the-Bowery

### Books

Adams III, Charles, *New York City Ghost Stories* (Reading, PA: Exeter House Books, 1996), 36–45.

Blackhall, Susan, *Ghosts of New York* (San Diego, Calif.: Thunder Bay Press, 2005), 31–33.

Hauck, Dennis William, *Haunted Places: The National Directory* (New York: Penguin Group (USA) Inc., 1994), 304.

Macken, Linda Lee, *Ghostly Gotham: New York City's Haunted History* (Forked River, NJ: Black Cat Press, 2002), 51.

Revai, Cheri, *Haunted New York City: Ghosts and Strange Phenomena of the Big Apple* (Mechanicsburg, PA: Stackpole Books, 2008), 45–47.

### Articles

Bryk, William, "A.T. Stewart's Grave Was Robbed, His Body Snatched," *New York Press* (October 30, 2001). www.nypress.com/article-4997-at-stewarts-grave-was-robbed-his-body-snatched.html.

### Other Web pages

www.stmarksbowery.org/history-test.html

# Chapter 10: St. Paul's Chapel

### Books

Blackhall, Susan, *Ghosts of New York* (San Diego, Calif.: Thunder Bay Press, 2005), 14–17.

Macken, Linda Lee, *Ghostly Gotham: New York City's Haunted History* (Forked River, NJ: Black Cat Press, 2002), 15.

Revai, Cheri, *Haunted New York City: Ghosts and Strange Phenomena of the Big Apple* (Mechanicsburg, PA: Stackpole Books, 2008), 53–56.

### Web pages

www.saintpaulschapel.org/about_us

# Chapter 11: Trinity Episcopal Church and Graveyard

### Books

Macken, Linda Lee, *Ghostly Gotham: New York City's Haunted History* (Forked River, NJ: Black Cat Press, 2002), 13–16.

### Web pages

www.trinitywallstreet.org/history/timeline

www.trinitywallstreet.org/news/articles/the-sonic-boon-new-organ-is-digital-realistic-and-powerful-but-is-it-sacred

# Chapter 12: Conference House

## Books

Blackman, W. Haden, *The Field Guide to North American Hauntings* (New York: Three Rivers Press, 1998), 11–13.

Revai, Cheri, *Haunted New York City: Ghosts and Strange Phenomena of the Big Apple* (Mechanicsburg, PA: Stackpole Books, 2008), 96–99.

## Public document

Bedell House Designation Report, New York City Landmarks Preservation Commission, April 12, 2005. www.nyc.gov/html/lpc/downloads/pdf/reports/bedellhouse.pdf.

## Other Web pages

www.conferencehouse.org/conf.html

# Chapter 13: Ellis and Liberty Islands

## Books

Printz, Thomas, *The Seven Mighty Elohim Speak On: The Seven Steps to Precipitation,* Ascended Master Teaching Foundation (Mount Shasta, Calif., 1986), xii–xiii. Reprint of the 1957 original.

## Articles

Claffey, Mike, "Leaper Dies At Liberty," *New York Daily News* (June 1, 1997). www.nydailynews.com/archives/news/1997/06/01/1997-06-01_leaper_dies_at_liberty.html.

Newman, Maria, and William K. Rashbaum,"Yankee Dies in Plane Crash, Official Says," *New York Times* (October 11, 2006). www.nytimes.com/2006/10/11/nyregion/12crashcnd.html.

"Curious ghost stories; bedlow's island was the scene of the adventures. How a search for capt. Kyd's buried treasure proved disastrous and how a live soldier ghost was captured -- incidents in connection with the cases related," *New York Times* (August 14, 1892), 15. http://query.nytimes.com/mem/archive-free/pdf?res=9B04E6DC1238E233A25757C1A96E9C94639ED7CF.

"Man Leaps to His Death From Statue of Liberty," Metro News Briefs, *New York Times* (June 2, 1997). www.nytimes.com/1997/06/02/nyregion/man-leaps-to-his-death-from-statue-of-liberty.html.

"Ghosts of Ellis Island," Opinion, *New York Times* (September 8, 2001).

Newman, Maria, "The Rust Must Go, But the Ghosts Linger; Restoring Ellis Island's Forgotten Side," *New York Times* (August 13, 2001). www.nytimes. com/2001/08/13/nyregion/the-rust-must-go-but-the-ghosts-linger-restoring-ellis-island-s-forgotten-side.html.

**Other Web pages**

"Dark Destinations" listing for the Statue of Liberty, www.thecabinet. com. www.thecabinet.com/darkdestinations/location.php?sub_id=dark_destinations&letter=s&location_id=the_statue_of_liberty

Ellis Island official Web site, National Park Service. www.nps.gov/elis/index.htm.

# Chapter 14: Richmond Town

**Books**

Revai, Cheri, *Haunted New York City: Ghosts and Strange Phenomena of the Big Apple* (Mechanicsburg, PA: Stackpole Books, 2008), 82–83.

**Articles**

"A life taken for a life; Edward Reinhardt hanged in Staten Island," *New York Times* (January 15, 1881). http://query.nytimes.com/mem/archive-free/pdf?res= 9905E6DE1730EE3ABC4D52DFB766838A699FDE.

**Other Web pages**

"Broom Magick," www.ravenandcrone.com/catalog/a39/Besoms-and-Brooms/article_info.html.

"Most Haunted Town/City in New York: Staten Island," www.unsolvedmysteries. com/usm391583.html.

www.scaredonline.com

# Chapter 15: Snug Harbor

**Books**

Revai, Cheri, *Haunted New York City: Ghosts and Strange Phenomena of the Big Apple* (Mechanicsburg, PA: Stackpole Books, 2008), 95.

**Web pages**

"Sailors' Snug Harbor," http://en.wikipedia.org/wiki/Sailors'_Snug_Harbor

www.snug-harbor.org

## Chapter 16: Van Cortlandt House

**Books**

Langan-Schmidt, Therese, Ghosts of New York City (Atglen, PA: Schiffer
   Publishing, 2003), 126–129.

**Articles**

Lii, Jane H., "Neighborhood Report: Van Cortlandt Park; 1748 Mansion Full of
   History but Needs $1 Million in TLC," *New York Times* (July 16, 1995). www.
   nytimes.com/1995/07/16/nyregion/neighborhood-report-van-cortlandt-park-
   1748-mansion-full-history-but-needs-1.html.

**Other Web pages**

www.historichousetrust.org/item.php?i_id=30

"Haunted Van Cortlandt Mansion," True Ghost Tales Paranormal Blog (May 25,
   2009). www.trueghosttales.com/paranormal/haunted-van-cortlandt-mansion.

www.vancortlandthouse.org

## Chapter 17: Alice Austen House

**Books**

Revai, Cheri, *Haunted New York City: Ghosts and Strange Phenomena of
   the Big Apple* (Mechanicsburg, PA: Stackpole Books, 2008), 85–86.

**Web pages**

"2008 Arsenal Gallery Exhibits," www.nycgovparks.org/sub_things_to_do/
   attractions/public_art/arsenal_gallery/2008_pages/2008_gallery_index.html.

"Alice Austen House Investigation," Paranormal Investigations of Staten Island.
   www.paranormal-investigations-of-staten-island.20fr.com/alice_austen.html

## Chapter 18: Garibaldi-Meucci Museum

### Books

Revai, Cheri, *Haunted New York City: Ghosts and Strange Phenomena of the Big Apple* (Mechanicsburg, PA: Stackpole Books, 2008), 93–95.

### Web pages

Garibaldi-Meucci Museum official Web site, www.garibaldimeuccimuseum.org.

"Garibaldi-Meucci Museum," Office of the Staten Island Borough President, www.statenislandusa.com/pages/garibaldi.html.

Staten Island Paranormal Society official Web site, siparanormalsociety.tripod.com/home.html.

## Chapter 19: Merchant's House Museum

### Books

Langan-Schmidt, Therese, *Ghosts of New York City* (Atglen, PA: Schiffer Publishing, 2003), 101.

Macken, Linda Lee, *Ghostly Gotham: New York City's Haunted History* (Forked River, NJ: Black Cat Press, 2002), 37–40.

## Chapter 20: Morris-Jumel Mansion

### Books

Adams III, Charles, *New York City Ghost Stories* (Reading, PA: Exeter House Books, 1996), 143–153.

Holzer, Hans, *Ghosts* (New York: Black Dog & Leventhal Publishers, Inc., 1997), 531–537.

Macken, Linda Lee, *Ghostly Gotham: New York City's Haunted History* (Forked River, NJ: Black Cat Press, 2002), 104–105.

## Chapter 21: Fort Wadsworth

### Books

Macken, Linda Lee, *Haunted History of Staten Island* (Forked River, NJ: Black Cat Press, 2000), 45.

## Articles

Cohen, Patricia, "He Sings the Borough Forgotten," *New York Times* (June 26, 2007). www.nytimes.com/2007/06/26/arts/design/26stat.html.

"100 Boy Refugees Flee Reservation," *New York Times* (September 8, 1920). http://query.nytimes.com/gst/abstract.html?res=990DEED61F31E03ABC4053DF BF66838B639EDE.

"Boy Refugee Slain; 75 Others Escape," New York Times (September 10, 1920). http://query.nytimes.com/gst/abstract.html?res=9405E5D61E3CEE3ABC4852DF BF66838B639EDE.

"The Cartridge Exploded.; A Serious Accident At Fort Wadsworth -- One Man Killed," *New York Times* (November 8, 1890). http://query.nytimes.com/gst/ abstract.html?res=9A06E2D8113BE533A2575BC0A9679D94619ED7CF.

"Killed in Mimic War," New York Times (June 20, 1908). http://query.nytimes.com/ gst/abstract.html?res=9C07EEDA1631E233A25753C2A9609C946997D6CF.

"Took His Own Life.; A Soldier In Fort Wadsworth, Staten Island, Shoots Himself," *New York Times* (October 11, 1891). http://query.nytimes.com/gst/abstract.ht ml?res=9C00E6DE123AE533A25752C1A9669D94609ED7CF.

## Video

"A Walk Around Staten Island with David Hartman and Historian Barry Lewis," WNET Thirteen New York. Video, www.thirteen.org/statenisland.

## Other Web pages

"Haunted Places in Staten Island," ParanormalKnowledge.com. www. paranormalknowledge.com/articles/haunted-places-in-staten-island.html.

Official Web site of the Staten Island Borough Historian, www. statenislandhistorian.com.

# Chapter 22: Washington Square Park

## Books

Cunningham, Scott, *The Complete Book of Incense, Oils, and Brews* (Woodbury, Minnesota: Llewellyn Publications, 1999), 45.

Revai, Cheri, *Haunted New York City: Ghosts and Strange Phenomena of the Big Apple* (Mechanicsburg, PA: Stackpole Books, 2008), 48–51.

Schoenberg, Dr. Phillip Ernest, *Ghosts of Manhattan: Legendary Spirits and Notorious Haunts*, Haunted America Series (Charleston, SC: The History Press, 2009), 72.

## Articles

Buck, Rinker, "Deaths Disturb a 'Dream College'," *Hartford* (CT) *Courant* (April 11, 2004). Reprinted at www.suicidereferencelibrary.com/test4.php?id=1139.

Carlson, Jenn, "Early Morning Suicide at NYU's Bobst Library," Gothamist.com (November 3, 2009). www.gothamist.com/2009/11/03/early_morning_bobst_suicide.php.

Cross, Heather, "Haunted New York City," About.com New York City Travel. http://gonyc.about.com/od/halloween/a/haunted_newyork.htm.

Katz, Celeste, "Suicides force NYU to put up barriers," *New York Daily News* (October 14, 2003). www.nydailynews.com/archives/news/2003/10/14/2003-10-14_suicides_force_nyu_to_put_up.html

Rosa, Paul, "The Triangle Shirtwaist Fire," HistoryBuff.com. www.historybuff.com/library/refshirtwaist.html.

Sun, Rebecca, and others, "N.Y.U. reacts to second Bobst leap within a month," *The Villager* (vol. 73, no. 24, October 15–21, 2003). www.thevillager.com/villager_25/nyureacts.html.

"Confirmed student death in Bobst this morning," *Washington Square News* (November 3, 2009). www.nyunews.com/news/2009/nov/03/death.

"Ghost Stories," *FCM Connected* (newsletter of the Facilities & Construction Management department of New York University), vol. 1, issue 2, August 2008. www.nyu.edu/fcm/pdfs/newsletter/June2008.pdf.

# Chapter 23: Woodlawn Cemetery

## Web page

www.thewoodlawncemetery.org

# Spotlight: Hart Island

## Books

Hunt, Melina, and Joel Sternfeld, *Hart Island: Discovery of an Unknown Territory* (New York: Scalo Publishers, 1998).

## Articles

Lueck, Thomas J., "Boat Believed Used by Four Lost Teenagers Is Found Capsized Near Hart Island," *New York Times* (February 2, 2003). www.nytimes.com/2003/02/02/nyregion/boat-believed-used-by-four-lost-teenagers-is-found-capsized-near-hart-island.html.

McFadden, Robert D., and Robert F. Worth, "Body Found Off City Island Is One of Four Missing Boys," *New York Times* (April 27, 2003). www.nytimes.com/2003/04/27/nyregion/body-found-off-city-island-is-one-of-four-missing-boys.html.

Nickel Jr., Richard, photoblog "Hart Island" (August 29, 2008) at blog *The Kingston Lounge*. http://kingstonlounge.blogspot.com/2008/08/hart-island.html.

Ortega, Ralph R., and Alice McQuillan, "Teen's Body Surfaces on Hart Island," *New York Daily News* (May 19, 2003). www.nydailynews.com/archives/news/2003/05/19/2003-05-19_teen_s_body_surfaces_on_hart.html

"A brief historical note on the Hart Island annual remembrance rite offered for all buried in Potter's Field," New York Correction History Society, www.correctionhistory.org/html/chronicl/hart/html/hartrite.html.

"Bobby Driscoll," Wikipedia.org. http://en.wikipedia.org/wiki/Bobby_Driscoll.

"Hart Island," *The Morning News*, October 10, 2002. www.themorningnews.org/archives/new_york_new_york/hart_island.php.

# Chapter 24: Belasco Theater

## Books

Blackhall, Susan, *Ghosts of New York* (San Diego, Calif.: Thunder Bay Press, 2005), 82–85.

Macken, Linda Lee, *Ghostly Gotham: New York City's Haunted History* (Forked River, NJ: Black Cat Press, 2002), 83–85.

Revai, Cheri, *Haunted New York: Ghosts and Strange Phenomena of the Empire State* (Mechanicsburg, PA: Stackpole Books, 2005), 85–86.

## Articles

Kanner, Leora, "Haunting Broadway: The Ghost of David Belasco," *Broadway Magazine*. www.broadway.tv/broadway-features-reviews/haunting-broadway-the-ghost-of-david-belasco.

Viagas, Robert, "Ghosts of Broadway," *Playbill* (10 Jun 2005). www.playbill.com/features/article/93486-The-Ghosts-of-Broadway.

**Other Web pages**

"David Belasco," Answers.com. www.answers.com/topic/belasco-david.

"David Belasco," Jewish Virtual Library. www.jewishvirtuallibrary.org/jsource/biography/Belasco.html.

"Belasco Theatre," New York City Landmarks Guide at www.jimsdeli.com/landmarks/42-51_w/belasco-theater.htm.

"Belasco Theatre," www.nycgo.com/?event=view.venuedetails&id=7645.

"NYC - 44th Street theater" (July 28, 2003), The Monstrous Forum. www.monstrous.com/forum/index.php?topic=228.0

# Spotlight: Theater Myths and Traditions

**Books**

Langan-Schmidt, Therese, *Ghosts of New York City* (Atglen, PA: Schiffer Publishing, 2003), 112.

**Articles**

Leber, Ariel, "Theater Superstitions and Traditions" (Web site for senior project at Upper Merion Area High School, 2006). www.theatersuperstition.bravehost.com/Classic.html.

Swingle, Sharon, "Ghosts and Ghost Lights" (Theater Superstitions Web site, 2005). www.siskiyous.edu/theatre/theatersuperstitions/ghostlight.htm.

"Theatre Lore: Where Does It Come From?", ArtsAlive.ca (educational Web site by Canada's National Arts Centre). www.artsalive.ca/en/eth/infozone/theatrelore.html.

# Chapter 25: Cherry Lane Theater

**Web pages**

Official Web site of the Cherry Lane Theatre, www.cherrylanetheatre.com.

# Chapter 26: New Amsterdam Theater

**Books**

Blackhall, Susan, *Ghosts of New York* (San Diego, Calif.: Thunder Bay Press, 2005), 70–75.

Macken, Linda Lee, *Ghostly Gotham: New York City's Haunted History* (Forked River, NJ: Black Cat Press, 2002), 91–93.

**Articles**

Long, Bruce, ed., *Taylorology: A Continuing Exploration of the Life and Death of William Desmond Taylor* (issue 33, September 1995). www.public. asu.edu/~ialong/Taylor33.txt.

Zur-Linden, W., "Antidotes for Bichloride of Mercury," *AJN: The American Journal of Nursing* (vol. 29, issue 3, March 1929), 262.

"Paris Authorities Investigate Death Of Olive Thomas," *New York Times* (September 11, 1920). http://query.nytimes.com/gst/abstract.html?res=9403E2 D61E3CEE3ABC4952DFBF66838B639EDE

**Other Web pages**

"New Amsterdam Theater," NewYorkCityTheater.com. www.newyorkcitytheatre. com/theaters/newamsterdamtheater/history.php.

# Chapter 27: Palace Theater

**Books**

Macken, Linda Lee, *Ghostly Gotham: New York City's Haunted History* (Forked River, NJ: Black Cat Press, 2002), 89.

**Articles**

Metheny, Pat, "The Life & Music of Jaco Pastorius," www.jacopastorius.com/ biography/life.asp.

Viagas, Robert, "Ghosts of Broadway," *Playbill* (10 Jun 2005). www.playbill.com/ features/article/93486-The-Ghosts-of-Broadway.

"Actress Arrested in Theater Chase," *New York Times* (August 11, 1914). http:// query.nytimes.com/gst/abstract.html?res=9803EFDC1430E733A25752C1A96E9C 946596D6CF

"The Ghost at NYC's Palace Theater," Phantoms & Monsters blog (December 22, 2008), http://naturalplane.blogspot.com/2008/12/ghost-at-nycs-palace-theater.html.

"The Palace Theater," HauntedHouses.com. www.hauntedhouses.com/states/ny/palace_theatre.cfm.

"Phantoms of the Palace Theatre," official Web site of Elizabeth Baron, www.elizabethbaron.com/palace.htm.

Profile of Jaco Pastorius at RottenTomatoes.com, www.rottentomatoes.com/celebrity/jaco_pastorius/biography.php.

# Spotlight: Times Square

### Books

Langan-Schmidt, Therese, *Ghosts of New York City* (Atglen, PA: Schiffer Publishing, 2003), 55–56.

### Web pages

"The Ghost Pilots of Times Square, retold by S. E. Schlosser," www.americanfolklore.net/folktales/ny12.html.

# Chapter 28 Paradise Theater

### Articles

Bridges, Elizabeth, "Historic Theater Reopens," *Mount Hope Monitor* (November 10, 2009). www.mounthopemonitor.org/?p=367.

Kugel, Seth, "Urban Tactics: For an Opulent Movie Palace, New Hope for a Revival," *New York Times* (August 3, 2003). www.nytimes.com/2003/08/03/nyregion/urban-tactics-for-an-opulent-movie-palace-new-hope-for-a-revival.html.

Roe, Ken, "Paradise Theater," Cinema Treasures Web site, www.cinematreasures.org/theater/900.

### Other Web pages

"History of The Paradise" at official Web site of the Paradise Theater, www.paradisetheaterevents.com/index.php?option=com_content&view=article&id=74&Itemid=78.

## Chapter 29: Public Theater

**Books**

Macken, Linda Lee, *Ghostly Gotham: New York City's Haunted History* (Forked River, NJ: Black Cat Press, 2002), 41–43.

## Spotlight: Radio City Music Hall

**Books**

Schoenberg, Dr. Phillip Ernest, *Ghosts of Manhattan: Legendary Spirits and Notorious Haunts*, Haunted America Series (Charleston, SC: The History Press, 2009), 111–112.

**Web pages**

"History," official Web site of Radio City Music Hall, www.radiocity.com/about/history.html.

## Chapter 30: Chelsea and Algonquin Hotels

**Books**

Blackhall, Susan, *Ghosts of New York* (San Diego, Calif.: Thunder Bay Press, 2005), 76–81.

**Articles**

Holden, Stephen, "Susannah McCorkle, Pop-Jazz Singer, Is Dead At 55," *New York Times* (May 21, 2001). www.nytimes.com/2001/05/20/obituaries/20MCCO.html.

Nyholm, Christine Bude, "Haunted Algonquin Hotel New York City," AssociatedContent.com. www.associatedcontent.com/article/386415/haunted_algonquin_hotel_new_york_city.html?cat=37.

Nyholm, Christine Bude, "Haunted Hotel Chelsea in New York," AssociatedContent.com. www.associatedcontent.com/article/402192/haunted_hotel_chelsea_in_new_york.html?cat=37.

Biography of Susannah McCorkle at her official Web site. http://susannahmccorkle.home.mindspring.com/bioSM.html.

### Other Web pages

"The Chelsea Hotel," www.ghost-story.co.uk/stories/chelseahotelghosts.html.

"Is NYC's Algonquin Hotel haunted? One guest says so . . ." Oyster.com Blog (October 30, 2009). http://blog.oyster.com/is-nycs-algonquin-hotel-haunted-one-guest-says-so-3707.

www.algonquinhotel.com

www.hotelchelsea.com

# Chapter 31: The Dakota

### Books

Adams III, Charles, *New York City Ghost Stories* (Reading, PA: Exeter House Books, 1996), 132–136.

Blackhall, Susan, *Ghosts of New York* (San Diego, Calif.: Thunder Bay Press, 2005), 90–97.

### Articles

Grimes, William, "A Gang of Ghosts Ready to Rumble," *New York Times* (October 29, 1993). www.nytimes.com/1993/10/29/arts/a-gang-of-ghosts-ready-to-rumble.html.

"Answers About Haunted New York," *New York Times* (October 29, 2007). http://cityroom.blogs.nytimes.com/2007/10/29/answers-about-haunted-new-york.

"The Dakota," description for Web site for New York University course "Architecture in New York: A Field Study," www.nyu.edu/classes/finearts/nyc/upperwest/dakota.html.

### Other Web pages

www.wollmanskatingrink.com/main_wollman.htm

# Chapter 32: Fordham University

### Books

Revai, Cheri, *Haunted New York City: Ghosts and Strange Phenomena of the Big Apple* (Mechanicsburg, PA: Stackpole Books, 2008), 4–5.

### Articles

Williams, Yona, "The Haunted Tales of Fordham University," Unexplainable.net (October 12, 2009). www.unexplainable.net/artman/publish/article_14016. shtml.

### Other Web pages

"Fordham Facts," www.fordham.edu/discover_fordham/facts_26604.asp.

"Haunted Places in New York," www.theshadowlands.net/places/newyork.htm.

## Spotlight: Various New York City Ghosts

### Books

Adams III, Charles, *New York City Ghost Stories* (Reading, PA: Exeter House Books, 1996), 137–140.

Blackhall, Susan, *Ghosts of New York* (San Diego, Calif.: Thunder Bay Press, 2005), 86–89.

Hauck, Dennis William, *Haunted Places: The National Directory* (New York: Penguin Group USA Inc., 1994), 304–305.

Macken, Linda Lee, *Ghostly Gotham: New York City's Haunted History* (Forked River, NJ: Black Cat Press, 2002), 79–80.

# Acknowledgments

I AM SO THANKFUL for and appreciative of the many people who helped me as I wrote this book. Professionally, first and foremost would be my editor, John Kachuba. Truly, this man has saved me from the perils of dangling participles and "writer's block" more times than I care to admit. Thank you also to my publisher, Jack Heffron, and to publicist Kara Pelicano, who work constantly to market and promote the *America's Haunted Road Trip* series.

I must thank paranormal authors and researchers Cheri Farnsworth, Lynda Lee Macken, Rosemary Ellen Guiley, Jeff Belanger, and John Zaffis. They have inspired me and encouraged me throughout this project. Honestly, writing a book is overwhelming at times; having these accomplished authors to cheer me on has been invaluable.

Thanks to all the proprietors, managers, bartenders, security guards and docents at the various places I investigated for this book. Their insights and knowledge added such value to these chapters. I especially want to thank Anthony Bellov of the Merchant House Museum, Adam Weprin and Joseph Kunst of the Bridge Café, Brian Backstrom of Snug Harbor, Kenneth Leslie of the Public Theater, Bonnie McCourt of the Garibaldi-Meucci Museum, and Dan Meharg of Fort Wadsworth.

I appreciate my team leaders at the New Jersey Ghost Hunters Society who have "held down the fort" while I've been consumed with writing. Dina Chirico's navigation skills on our Bronx adventure were worth her weight in gold. Thanks also to fellow ghosthunter Brian Cano of *Scared!* He was a great resource for the Richmond Town chapter, and Amy Raiola of the Staten Island Paranormal Society for their investigative work at the Garibaldi-Meucci Museum.

I owe special thanks to my mom. Without her knowledge of the Broadway area and the New Jersey Transit bus and train schedules, I would have been completely lost. Thanks to Dad, too, for providing bus stop round trip transfers for Mom and me. Mom, Dad, I can never thank you both enough—for everything.

Thank you to my sons, Brian and Trent, who were by my side ghosthunting at many of the locations in this book. They endured drive-thru food, frantic U-turns and my hysterical arguments with Tom-Tom, the GPS unit.

Finally, thanks to all my friends on Facebook, MySpace, and Yahoo. Many of you I've never met in person, but your support and your recommendations for haunted sites have been tremendous. I'm sure we'll cross paths in person at some upcoming ghost or paranormal convention; then I can thank you personally.

# About the Author

L'AURA HLADIK's interest in the paranormal started in childhood and culminated with living in an actual haunted rental house when she was in the eighth grade. In 1993, she officially began hunting for ghosts, and in 1998 she founded the New Jersey Ghost Hunters Society (www.njghs .net), currently the largest paranormal investigating organization in the state with over 700 members.

L'Aura is also the author of *Ghosthunting New Jersey*, another book in the *America's Haunted Road Trip* series. She enjoys presenting her findings in multimedia presentations to libraries and civic organizations. L'Aura has appeared on the nationally syndicated talk show *Montel Williams* as well as local cable television shows and various AM and FM radio stations.

Although L'Aura's ghost research takes her beyond New Jersey and New York City to other states (and even other countries, such as Ireland), the "Jersey Girl" always comes home to her favorite haunt.